The Origin and Meaning of the Ancient Characters of Style

Analecta Gorgiana

383

Series Editor
George Anton Kiraz

Analecta Gorgiana is a collection of long essays and short monographs which are consistently cited by modern scholars but previously difficult to find because of their original appearance in obscure publications. Carefully selected by a team of scholars based on their relevance to modern scholarship, these essays can now be fully utilized by scholars and proudly owned by libraries.

The Origin and Meaning of the Ancient Characters of Style

George Hendrickson

gorgias press

2009

Gorgias Press LLC, 180 Centennial Ave., Piscataway, NJ, 08854, USA

www.gorgiaspress.com

Copyright © 2009 by Gorgias Press LLC

Originally published in

All rights reserved under International and Pan-American Copyright Conventions. No part of this publication may be reproduced, stored in a retrieval system or transmitted in any form or by any means, electronic, mechanical, photocopying, recording, scanning or otherwise without the prior written permission of Gorgias Press LLC.

2009

ISBN 978-1-60724-632-9

ISSN 1935-6854

Extract from *The American Journal of Philology* 26 (1905)

Printed in the United States of America

AMERICAN JOURNAL OF PHILOLOGY

Vol. XXVI, 3.   Whole No. 103.

I.—THE ORIGIN AND MEANING OF THE ANCIENT CHARACTERS OF STYLE.

Cicero, in the third book de Oratore, pleading for an ideal union of philosophy statesmanship and eloquence in the person of the orator—a union such as he finds exemplified in the sophists of fifth century Greece—describes with much picturesqueness the divorce of the arts of thought and speech, which before had been one under the common name of philosophy.[1] As such a unit Gorgias Thrasymachus and Isocrates had conceived of their field and instructed their pupils. But Socrates, though himself a product of this comprehensive conception and a type of the versatile skill which it produced, had brought in division and usurped for the science of thought that designation which thinkers orators, and statesmen had before enjoyed in common. Hence arose a division almost as of soul and body, so that the teaching of thought and expression was no longer one and the same.

The sharp outlines of the antithesis as described by Cicero do not in the widest sense correspond to the historical development as it can be traced;[2] they do, however, agree essentially with such pictures as the Gorgias and the Phaedrus present, in which, in concrete and almost plastic form, we have set over

---

[1] De Or. III 56: hanc cogitandi pronuntiandique rationem vimque dicendi veteres Graeci sapientiam nominabant. Ib. 60: cum nomine appellarentur uno, quod omnis rerum optimarum cognitio atque in eis exercitatio philosophia nominaretur. See also 60 and 61 for the text following.

[2] See von Arnim, Dio von Prusa (Berlin, 1898), ch. 1.

against each other the two rival arts, dialectic (philosophy) and rhetoric, and the beginnings of that hostility which in one form or another—and in spite of many efforts at reconciliation, such as Cicero's—continued down to late antiquity.[1] The rhetoricians, looking upon themselves as the heirs of the early sophists, still claimed 'philosophy' as the proper designation of their activity, and on the other hand the philosophers were fond of indicating the nature and scope of a true or ideal rhetoric.

Of such attempts the earliest, and in its wide-reaching influence the most important, is that contained in the latter part of the Phaedrus. It is of course no more than an outline, drawn with conscious antithesis to the rhetorical treatises of the contemporary sophists—Theodorus Gorgias Thrasymachus and others.[2] First of all, the foundations of the art will consist of the same capacity for exact logical analysis and synthesis, based upon a true knowledge of things, as is demanded of the dialectician (266 AB, 260 D, 262 A). But oratory is the art of enchanting the soul ($\psi v \chi a \gamma \omega \gamma i a$), and therefore to the dialectical attainments before enumerated, must be added a genuine knowledge of human souls, their varieties, differences, susceptibilities, etc. (271 D). Thus the true rhetorician will strive to do by reasoned method that which the sophistical rhetoric had sought to teach by mechanical rules or by the mere example of passages to be learned. But in this sketch of a 'true rhetoric' no mention is made of a special doctrine of style—nor need we wonder. For in spite of the fact that among the resources for the attainment of the $\psi v \chi a \gamma \omega \gamma i a$, at which all aimed, purely stylistic means—the Gorgianic figures, rhythm, etc.—played a most important rôle, yet it does not appear that a special doctrine of style apart from invention and arrangement had yet been formulated.[3] For the separation of matter or thought ($\pi \rho \acute{a} \gamma \mu a \tau a$) from the forms of expression is not an easy abstraction. In the pre-Aristotelian rhetoric the division of the subject was concrete, based upon the oration itself—prooemium, narrative, argument, epilogue, and under each of these heads all the necessary instruction was

---

[1] De Or. III 72: postea dissociati, ut exposui, a Socrate diserti a doctis . . . philosophi eloquentiam despexerunt, oratores sapientiam.

[2] On the nature of the $\tau \acute{\epsilon} \chi \nu \eta$ $\dot{\rho} \eta \tau o \rho \iota \kappa \acute{\eta}$ of the sophists see the suggestive discussion of Gercke in Hermes 32 (1897), pp. 341–359.

[3] Cf. Gercke l. c. p. 355.

contained, belonging more or less indistinguishably in part to invention and in part to style.

The outlines which Plato affords we find carried out in detailed treatment by Aristotle.[1] The Platonic points of view (apart from some rather essential differences of conception as to the relation of dialectic and rhetoric to philosophy as a whole) are absolved in the first two books of the Rhetoric as it has come down to us.[2] In book I Aristotle aims to establish a new foundation for rhetoric, which shall make of it as exact an instrument of proof as the practical uses of the art admit of. Argument is to be conducted by enthymeme and example, which are merely forms of the syllogism and induction of dialectic. Rhetoric is therefore essentially a form of dialectic,[3] adapted to the conditions which are imposed upon it by the nature of the audience to which it appeals. The proofs are the essential thing and enthymemes are the very heart of proof (σῶμα τῆς πίστεως). The most efficient orator accordingly will be the one most skilled in enthymemes (1355 a, 3-14). The technicians therefore who pay no attention to the treatment of the proofs nor to the resources by which one may become skilled in enthymemes (1354 b, 21), and who devote themselves to other things, such as the nature of prooemiums, narratives, etc., have devoted themselves to things which are apart from the actual issue (τὰ ἔξω τοῦ πράγματος).

[1] Spengel, Über die Rhetorik des Aristoteles. Abhlg. d. Münch. Akad. 1851.
[2] Book I deals essentially with the peculiarly Aristotelian adaptation of dialectic to the purposes of rhetoric, the construction in short of a rhetorical dialectic, while book II discusses the psychological basis of the appeal outside of the facts (τὰ ἔξω τοῦ πράγματος)—the ψυχαγωγία of the Phaedrus. That the Aristotelian definition of rhetoric does not contemplate a doctrine of style was noted by Quintilian (II 15, 13 nihil nisi inventionem complectitur). It has further been observed that in the first two books there are no anticipatory references to book III and that this book is not included in the distribution of matter made at either the beginning of book I or II, while on the other hand in the portion of book III περὶ λέξεως (1-12) there are no references to the two preceding books except at the beginning. For the whole matter see Marx, Aristoteles' Rhetorik, Berichte d. sächs. Akad. phil. hist. kl. vol. 52 (1900) p. 241 ff. If we add that the catalogue of Diogenes Laert. names the Rhetoric as consisting of only two books, it will seem very probable that books I and II presented what was meant to be a complete theory of rhetoric, without giving any place to a doctrine of style whatsoever.
[3] The various terms by which Aristotle designates this relation are: ἀντίστροφος (τῇ διαλεκτικῇ) 'corresponding' or 'parallel,' I 1 init.; παραφυές 'offshoot,' I 2, 1356 a, 25 ; μόριόν τι καὶ ὁμοία (ὁμοίωμα) 1356 a, 31.

Their aim is to put the judge (or audience) in a certain frame of mind favorable to their cause, irrespective of proof. That this is a matter of importance for the orator Aristotle does not deny; "for we give very different judgments under the influence of pain or pleasure, love or hate" (1356 a, 15): his criticism is that the technicians look to this and this only in their treatises (16). That it is a legitimate part of rhetoric he concedes, and promises to take it up in detail when he comes to speak περὶ τῶν παθῶν. This sharp contrast in point of view between Aristotle and his predecessors is summarized briefly near the beginning of the treatise (1354 a, 13): the proofs are the only artistic (ἔντεχνον) aspects of rhetoric; all else is surplusage.[1] The two points of view may be summed up in the words with which the πάθη—the extraneous matter to the treatment of which the earlier technicians had devoted themselves—are characterized (1354 a, 17):

(1) οὐ περὶ τοῦ πράγματός ἐστιν,
(2) ἀλλὰ πρὸς τὸν δικαστήν.

To both of these considerations Aristotle aims to contribute something new: to the first (περὶ τοῦ πράγματος) by outlining a method of dialectical proof, which earlier theorists had wholly neglected; to the second (πρὸς τὸν δικαστήν) by basing the appeal to the audience upon an accurate analysis of the characters of men and their emotions, in place of the empirical precepts (or examples) which the rhetoricians had indicated for each part of the oration.

If the Rhetoric were a work of perfect symmetry and co-ordination of parts ('aus einem Guss,' as Brandis said) we might have expected that the portion of the third book which deals with style should correspond to the main outlines of the two preceding books. In such case it would have been conceivable, or even natural, that a differentiation of style should have been made corresponding to the two divisions of the argument which we have observed, viz.: a stylistic form suited to proof or demonstration, and a second having regard to that which lies outside

[1] That Aristotle has with some inconsistency over-emphasized the significance of enthymeme for rhetorical proof Marx (l. c. p. 289) points out, showing that, if he here be taken strictly at his word, the doctrine of ἤθη and πάθη is excluded from the πίστεις ἔντεχνοι. Marx uses this inconsistency as evidence for his theory of the Rhetoric as an ὑπόμνημα σχολικόν.

the actual proof, and looking to an 'ethical' or emotional effect upon the listener or judge.

Aristotle recognizes that both declamation and style as employed in practical rhetoric in his time are significant chiefly because of the debased character of the audience (διὰ τὴν τοῦ ἀκροατοῦ μοχθηρίαν) and are therefore instruments for the perversion of justice. Strict justice (δίκαιον) demands that the question at issue should be settled on the merits of the case itself (αὐτοῖς τοῖς πράγμασι); for everything apart from the strict proof is really superfluous. This applies most to declamation, but in a less degree to style also; for differences in the mode of expression have some effect on the actual communication of the thought (πρὸς τὸ δηλῶσαι), but not so much as is commonly believed, and in fact the devices of style are a mere display and look to an effect upon the listener (ἀλλ' ἅπαντα φαντασία ταῦτ' ἐστὶ καὶ πρὸς τὸν ἀκροατήν): no one has ever thought of teaching geometry in such a fashion. Style (as also delivery) should in strict justice aim at nothing more than neither to give pain nor pleasure (τὸ δίκαιον μηδὲν πλείω ζητεῖν περὶ τὸν λόγον ἢ ὡς μήτε λυπεῖν μήτ' εὐφραίνειν 1404 a, 4).[1] Such a style, a fitting instrument for the ἐνθυμηματικός of book one, had Aristotle chosen to outline it, would have looked solely to the argument, and would have been the stylistic counterpart of the πίστεις ἐν αὐτῷ τῷ πράγματι. But this he has not done (perhaps because he deemed an art of mere plain speaking superfluous) and he proceeds in the subsequent chapters to set forth a theory of style which conforms in general to the standards of Isocratean prose—a theory which frankly looks beyond mere perspicuity to an emotional effect upon the listener. It is πρὸς τὸν ἀκροατήν.

That such is the case will not perhaps be immediately conceded, and it may be argued that the first requisite of style which Aristotle demands is clearness. To be sure if he demanded clearness and clearness only (as has been commonly said of his stylistic theory)[2] every requisite of a pragmatic unemotional style would be met. But it will be observed that in his definition of the excel-

---

[1] That is, the emotional element or appeal should be entirely eliminated, for this is the agency which distorts judgment and affords the basis for the perversion of the facts. See II 1, 1378 a, 20 ἔστι δὲ τὰ πάθη δι' ὅσα μεταβάλλοντες διαφέρουσι πρὸς τὰς κρίσεις, οἷς ἕπεται λύπη καὶ ἡδονή κτλ. and I 2, 1356 a, 15 οὐ γὰρ ὁμοίως ἀποδίδομεν τὰς κρίσεις λυπούμενοι καὶ χαίροντες κτλ.

[2] See the writer's paper on The Peripatetic Mean of Style, etc. in A. J. P. XXV (1904) p. 129.

lence of style,[1] while clearness is, to be sure, the first quality named, it is yet named merely as indispensable to the function of language as a means of communication, and so preliminary to any other desirable qualities. These are covered by the second demand that style shall be appropriate (πρέπουσαν). This relationship of the two parts of the definition appears most clearly from the similar definition of the excellence of style in the Poetics (ch. 22 init.): 'The perfection of style is to be clear and not mean. The style which uses only common or proper words is in the highest degree clear; at the same time it is mean,' i. e. not appropriate. Indeed, as the appropriate in Aristotle's definition of style is the category under which most of his observations looking to embellishment fall, so also is it the doorway through which distortion or perversion of the abstract truth is admitted to rhetoric. 'A style which is appropriate . . . invests the subject with persuasive efficacy. For the mind is cheated into a persuasion that the orator is speaking with sincerity, because under such circumstances men stand affected in that manner: so that people suppose things to be even as the speaker states them, what though in reality they are not'.[2]

As the ideal of argument and adjudication is to rest upon the merits of the case, so the ideal form of expression in such a controversy would be to seek nothing more than a colorless objectivity in stylistic form, evoking neither pain nor pleasure, like a demonstration in geometry. In such a style intelligibility would be the only consideration, though from an artistic point of view the language might not be appropriate, but mean; that is, the language of the speaker might in no wise conform to the magnitude or emotional significance of the issue at stake.[3]

In such considerations there are suggested two aspects of language which might have afforded a truly generic analysis

---

[1] Rhet. III 2 ὡρίσθω λέξεως ἀρετὴ σαφῆ εἶναι (σημεῖον γὰρ ὅτι ὁ λόγος ὡς ἐὰν μὴ δηλοῖ οὐ ποιήσει τὸ ἑαυτοῦ ἔργον) καὶ μήτε ταπεινὴν μήτε ὑπὲρ τὸ ἀξίωμα, ἀλλὰ πρέπουσαν.

[2] Rhet. III 7, 1408 a, 19 ff. (Oxford Translation).

[3] The late rhetoricians are fond of reducing passages of the orators marked by great feeling to their bare intellectual content for the sake of illustrating the orator's power. See for example the treatment of the famous oath in the De Corona in the treatise on the Sublime, ch. 16. Cicero, in Brutus 115, says of the defense of Rutilius Rufus by Q. Mucius Scaevola, that he spoke enucleate et polite ut solebat, nequaquam autem ea vi atque copia quam genus illud iudicii et magnitudo causae postulabat.

of style: (1) language as an objective colorless medium for the statement of fact or the expression of thought (πράγματα), and (2) language as a means of conveying (in addition to or as a part of the abstract thought) the color of the speaker's emotion or artistic feeling to his audience (πρὸς τὸν ἀκροατήν). The attitude of Aristotle toward language of the latter type is not one of hostility to it as such—rather it is one of sympathetic appreciation; it is only that, realizing its power, he deprecates the use of it as an instrument for the adjudication of questions of fact or right.

Such hints of a fundamental analysis of style, or perhaps more specific utterances of Aristotle elsewhere, were the source of a division of language with reference to its end or purpose which Theophrastus made. The fragment is cited by Ammonius[1] and is as follows: Διττῆς γὰρ οὔσης τῆς τοῦ λόγου σχέσεως, καθὰ διώρισεν ὁ φιλόσοφος Θεόφραστος, τῆς τε πρὸς τοὺς ἀκροωμένους, οἷς καὶ σημαίνει τι, καὶ τῆς πρὸς τὰ πράγματα, ὑπὲρ ὧν ὁ λέγων πεῖσαι προτίθεται τοὺς ἀκροωμένους, περὶ μὲν τὴν σχέσιν αὐτοῦ τὴν πρὸς τοὺς ἀκροατὰς καταγίνονται ποιητικὴ καὶ ῥητορική. διόπερ ἔργον αὐταῖς ἐκλέγεσθαί τε τὰ σεμνότερα τῶν ὀνομάτων, ἀλλὰ μὴ τὰ κοινὰ καὶ δεδημευμένα, καὶ ταῦτα ἐναρμονίως συμπλέκειν ἀλλήλοις, ὥστε διὰ τούτων καὶ τῶν τούτοις ἑπομένων, οἷον σαφηνείας γλυκύτητος καὶ τῶν ἄλλων ἰδεῶν ἔτι τε μακρολογίας καὶ βραχυλογίας, κατὰ καιρὸν πάντων παραλαμβανομένων, ἧσαί τε τὸν ἀκροατὴν καὶ ἐκπλῆξαι καὶ πρὸς τὴν πειθὼ χειρωθέντα ἔχειν. τῆς δέ γε πρὸς τὰ πράγματα τοῦ λόγου σχέσεως ὁ φιλόσοφος προηγουμένως ἐπιμελήσεται τό τε ψεῦδος διελέγχων καὶ τὸ ἀληθὲς ἀποδεικνύς, κτλ.

'Language is divided into two types, according to the philosopher Theophrastus, the one having reference to the hearers, the other to the matter concerning which the speaker aims to convince his audience. To the division with reference to the hearers belong poetry and rhetoric. Therefore its function is to choose the more stately words, and not those which are common or vulgar, and to interweave them with each other harmoniously, to the end that, by means of them and the effects which result from the employment of them, such as vividness, sweetness and other qualities of style, together with studied expansion and contraction, all employed at the suitable moment, the listener shall be charmed and moved and, with respect to intellectual persuasion, overmastered. The division looking to the matter

[1] In Aristotelis De Interpretatione Com. p. 65, 31 (ed. Berol. 1897).

will be the especial concern of the philosopher, refuting the false and setting forth the true'.

From the fundamental nature of this division it would seem that it may have formed a part of the introductory considerations to the treatise περὶ λέξεως.[1] But though it may have been found there, yet it is probable (as is suggested by the fragment itself as well as by the character of the other attested fragments) that Theophrastus, like Aristotle, only discussed in detail the λόγος πρὸς τοὺς ἀκροωμένους—language in its artistic aspects. The λόγος πρὸς τὰ πράγματα was adduced to mark off the whole territory of λέξις, but I see no evidence to show that it was a subject of further treatment. I have spoken of this analysis as generic, and it perhaps will be right to name as species under the first class ποιητική and ῥητορική which are assigned to it. In the second division, however, it would seem that the genus scarcely admits of subdivision into species. Philosophy is adduced as one of the most important (προηγουμένως ἐπιμελήσεται) fields for the employment of the λόγος πρὸς τὰ πράγματα, but it is only as an illustration, which might have been drawn from any other conceivable subject-matter:[2] the reference is to language as an objective medium for the statement of fact or thought, wherever and by whomsoever used.[3]

That there is a hint of this analysis of language in Aristotle has been shown, and it will be noted too that the names with which the two stylistic forms are designated—πρὸς τὰ πράγματα and πρὸς τοὺς ἀκροωμένους—correspond essentially to the two aspects of proof

---

[1] To which it is assigned by M. Schmidt, De Theophrasto rhetore, Halle, 1839 (Progr.), but it is not alluded to by Rabe, De Theophrasti libris περὶ λέξεως, Bonn, 1889 (Diss.).

[2] It will be recalled that Aristotle contrasts the usual language of rhetoric (πρὸς τὸν ἀκροατήν) with the method of presentation in geometry (III 1, 1404 a, 11).

[3] The fragment is commented on briefly by Prantl (Gesch. d. Logik, vol. I p. 351) who seems to have seen in it a deeper philosophical meaning than it contains, and he assumes that the distinction here drawn is between the Peripatetic true logic or apodeictic, and dialectic. Zeller notes his error and corrects it II³ 2 p. 821, and he further observes very justly (ib. 867 n. 4) that Theophrastus refers merely to stylistic form and in no sense contemplates an exhaustive distinction between rhetoric and poetry on the one hand and philosophy on the other. One other allusion to the fragment is cited by Busse (the editor of Ammonius) from an unpublished source, p. XXIII of his edition. It uses the analysis of Theophrastus to characterize the style of the De Interpretatione.

which Aristotle recognized: the pragmatic or dialectical (ἐν αὐτῷ τῷ πράγματι), and that which lies outside of the facts and looks to an emotional effect upon the judge or listener (πρὸς τὸν δικαστήν, ἀκροατήν). It is in the explicit recognition of a type of language or style corresponding to the pragmatic aspects of proof, and in the sharp separation of this from the artistic and emotional aspect of language, that Theophrastus has advanced beyond his master. It is, however, to be observed that, on the evidence of our fragment at least, the λόγος πρὸς τὰ πράγματα is not assigned a function in rhetoric, and that in this respect again there is agreement with Aristotle. For just as the latter merely suggests that it would be right in judicial disputes to employ an entirely colorless style, allowing the case to be fought out on its merits (τοῖς πράγμασι ἀγωνίζεσθαι), and yet proceeds to set forth a theory of artistic prose, so Theophrastus, while defining a pragmatic style, yet assigns rhetoric as a whole to the λόγος πρὸς τοὺς ἀκροωμένους. The position is obviously not wholly logical. For when once a method of strict objective argument had been devised for rhetoric it would seem natural that a corresponding doctrine of style should follow it. But it may be that Theophrastus, with discerning vision, recognized the impossibility of ever applying to practical rhetoric the rigorous demands of pragmatic proof which Aristotle had outlined; that it was useless to hope for a treatment of any part of rhetoric which did not look beyond the abstract argument to an emotional effect upon the listener. Such at all events seem to be the implications of the place to which rhetoric is assigned in our fragment, and they are confirmed by the dictates of historical observation and practical sense.

But the matter was not to rest here, and the pragmatic style which Theophrastus had defined was destined soon to claim the place in rhetoric which logically belonged to it from the Aristotelian analysis of the kinds of proof. With the growing influence of philosophy on Greek education and life, which is one of the chief characteristics of the third and second centuries B. C., more and more attention was given to the strictly logical phases of rhetoric. The Stoics especially with much acuteness (in spite of their pedantry and scholasticism) developed out of the Peripatetic apodeictic and dialectic a practical logic available for the demands of every-day life,[1] and in rhetoric they found the widest field for its

[1] See Steinthal, Geschichte der Sprachwissenschaft, vol. I p. 279 ff.

application. At their hands the dialectical aspects of rhetorical proof, which Aristotle had inaugurated, received minute attention, and particular rules for its application to every conceivable type of case or situation were formulated. Their results were, it seems certain, the chief source of Hermagoras' doctrine of invention, and through him they passed into the common body of rhetorical precept which the earliest post-Aristotelian treatises present. Rhetorical proof was conceived of as a problem or investigation (ζήτημα is the term of Hermagoras), and rhetoric made claim to the territory of exact demonstration. The point of view is characteristic for the mental attitude of the period of Hermagoras and the century antecedent to him, in which nearly all intellectual activity bears the stamp of scientific method, or at least of a striving after it. That such methods aimed at an ideal of more exact argument and adjudication, and sought to carry into effect the higher purposes of rhetoric which Aristotle had conceived cannot blind us to the futility of the effort, at a period when the intellectual strength of antiquity was beginning to wane, to replace the persuasion of eloquence by the persuasion of logical reasoning.[1] In spite of the influence of the Stoics and the great popularity which the system of Hermagoras enjoyed for a time, rhetoric continued to be, as it had always been, primarily an instrument of emotional appeal.

But this traditional and, in the ultimate analysis, essential aspect of rhetoric was in large measure excluded from early Stoic treatment by the general doctrine of ἀπάθεια which dominated their whole philosophy. That, in fact, as well as in theory the Stoics endeavored to realize their ideal of close reasoning and plain speaking, is evinced by many concrete examples, one of which in the person of the noble Rutilius Rufus will confront us later.

From a stylistic point of view their position corresponded to the minute attention which they paid to pragmatic proof, and to their repudiation of the emotional features of rhetoric. Their doctrine of style was in fact an elaboration of the λόγος πρὸς τὰ πράγματα. Its first quality was correctness and purity of the *conversational* idiom (as opposed to the poetical and elaborated style of conventional rhetoric[2]) :—Ἑλληνισμὸς μὲν οὖν ἐστι φράσις ἀδιάπτωτος

[1] See the excellent characterization of the relation of Hermagoras' rhetoric to the tendencies of the time, in Thiele's Hermagoras, pp. 24–27.
[2] Cf. Demetrius 77 (in description of the χαρακτὴρ μεγαλοπρεπής): τὴν δὲ λέξιν περιττὴν εἶναι δεῖ καὶ ἐξηλλαγμένην καὶ ἀσυνήθη μᾶλλον· . . . ἡ δὲ κυρία καὶ συνήθης σαφὴς μέν, λειτὴ δὲ καὶ εὐκαταφρόνητος. Cf. Poetics ch. 22 init.

ἐν τῇ τεχνικῇ καὶ μὴ εἰκαίᾳ συνηθείᾳ. Next clearness, aiming merely at the exact representation of the thought:—σαφήνεια δέ ἐστι λέξις γνωρίμως παριστᾶσα τὸ νοούμενον. Third brevity, limiting utterance to just that which was necessary to set forth the matter: συντομία δέ ἐστι λέξις αὐτὰ τὰ ἀναγκαῖα περιέχουσα πρὸς δήλωσιν τοῦ πράγματος. Fourth appropriateness, but not the λέξις πρέπουσα of the wide range which we have found in Aristotle, not an appropriateness looking to the character of the audience, the speaker, the occasion, etc.,[1] but merely of the word to the thing:—πρέπον δέ ἐστι λέξις οἰκεία τῷ πράγματι.[2] Positive ornament their system does not inculcate, at most only avoidance of the vulgar (the εἰκαία συνήθεια) —κατασκευὴ δέ ἐστι λέξις ἐκπεφευγυῖα τὸν ἰδιωτισμόν.[3] In all of these definitions the emphasis, or rather exclusive attention, which is given to the function of language purely as a means of expressing thought—γνωρίμως παριστᾶσα τὸ νοούμενον, πρὸς δήλωσιν τοῦ πράγματος, οἰκεία τῷ πράγματι—reveals its affinity with Theophrastus' λόγος πρὸς τὰ πράγματα. It is probable too that the stress which is laid upon grammatical purity and correctness, under Ἑλληνισμός, has its origin in the same desire to make language an *exact* vehicle of expression, not *loose* as might be the tendency of ordinary colloquial speech (ἐν τῇ τεχνικῇ καὶ μὴ εἰκαίᾳ συνηθείᾳ).[4]

Whether the early Stoic rhetoric paid any attention to other forms of proof than the πίστεις ἐν αὐτῷ τῷ πράγματι it is impossible

---

[1] It is defined by Dionysius de Lysia 9 as having reference πρός τε τὸν λέγοντα καὶ πρὸς τοὺς ἀκούοντας καὶ πρὸς τὸ πρᾶγμα, with manifest reference to the Aristotelian analysis of the πίστεις. Still more comprehensively by Cic. de Or. III 212, Or. 71 and 123. Cf. Arist. Poetics 25, 1461 a, 5.

[2] The exaggerated attention paid to κυριολογία, proprietas verborum, in the Stoic rhetoric (and its descendants) is the practical manifestation of this precept. It came at times to absorb almost the whole attention of stylists and literary students. Gellius and Fronto are for us the chief priests of the cult, but it goes far back of them and was a characteristic trait of all the Roman Atticists. See Fronto p. 62 ff. (Naber).

[3] The definitions are found in Diog. Laert. (life of Zeno) VII 59. It is now generally agreed that they are derived from Diogenes of Babylon. Cf. Schepss, De Soloecismo p. 23 and Reitzenstein, M. Terentius Varro, etc., (Leipz., 1901) in the addenda. It is probably early Stoic theory of style which is found in Varro (in a passage defending the Stoic standpoint of anomaly against analogy) L. L. VIII 26: the purpose (finis) of language is utilitas and its only virtues are clearness and brevity. Words have no other use than as the symbols of things cum utilitatis causa verba ideo sint imposita rebus ut eas significant. For other indications of the stylistic point of view of Stoicism see Quint. XI 3, 10 and esp. XII 10, 40.

[4] See Cicero De Or. III 49 init.

to say with certainty. It is likely, however, that it did not.¹ But in the Peripatetic school, so far as attention was paid to rhetoric at all, the Aristotelian division of the πίστεις continued to be the prevailing one, and from this source is derived the analysis of the *officia oratoris* which most later treatises present. Aristotle's analysis admits of interpretation as either twofold or threefold. It may be looked upon either as defining the proofs contained in the subject-matter itself and those outside of it (τὰ ἔξω τῶν πραγμάτων) or the latter again may be subdivided into ἤθη and πάθη. The threefold definition of the *officia oratoris* into *docere, conciliare, movere*, corresponding to a conception of the Aristotelian division as threefold, is the form in which the matter is best known. It is first found to my knowledge in Cicero de Oratore II 115, and its subsequent occurrence (in Quintilian and later Roman rhetoric) seems to be due to this source.

But of earlier date and wider diffusion is the interpretation of Aristotle as affording a twofold division; and this in fact is the more logical one. For even in the case of the threefold division of Cicero, it appears from several passages that the three functions are in reality thought of as two.² To such a division Quintilian alludes in expressing his preference for the Ciceronian threefold analysis: haec enim clarior divisio quam eorum qui totum opus in *res* et *adfectus* partiuntur (III 5, 2).³

---

¹ Cf. Quint. V pref. 1: fuerunt et clari quidem auctores, quibus solum videretur oratoris officium docere : namque et adfectus duplici ratione excludendos putabant, etc. The point of view is obviously Stoic. It may be demonstrated by comparison with the utterances of Rutilius Rufus in Cic. de Or. I 227.

² De Or. II 114 and esp. 178.

³ Cf. Apsines, Spengel I², p. 297, 2 εἰς δύο γὰρ εἴδη ὁ πᾶς λόγος διαιρεῖται ... τό τε πραγματικὸν καὶ τὸ παθητικόν. It is used by the Anon. Seguerianus (Spg. I², p. 357, 9 ff.) in a way to show with especial clearness its relation to Aristotle: οὐ γὰρ ἀεὶ προοιμιαστέον. ὅταν γὰρ μὴ πάθος ἔχῃ τὰ πράγματα οὐ προοιμιαστέον. . . . (23) δεύτερον, ὅταν πάθος μὲν ἔχῃ, ὁ δὲ ἀκροατὴς μὴ προσίηται τὸν ἔξω τῶν πραγμάτων λόγον ἤτοι σπεύδων ἢ ὀργιζόμενος. Again, p. 378, 17 (of the πίστεις ἔντεχνοι) εἴδη δὲ αὐτῶν δύο, τό τε ἀπὸ τοῦ πάθους καὶ τὸ ἀπὸ τοῦ πράγματος. Dionysius nowhere, I think, expressly defines the officia oratoris, but his language in several places reveals that he conceives of them as two. Dem. 4 τὸ διδάξαι and τὸ καταπλήξασθαι; ib. 44 ἀπάτη καὶ ψυχαγωγία and διδαχὴ καὶ ὠφέλεια. So also the Auct. ad Herenn. II. 29, 46: item vitiosum est id *augere* quod convenit *docere*, and implicitly in many other places. It was such a division which Cicero found in the Academic-Peripatetic source of his Part. Orat. where in 5 invention is thus distributed: ut inveniat (orator) quem ad

We have already seen that the Stoics had developed a stylistic doctrine corresponding to the pragmatic argumentation to which their rhetoric chiefly looked, a stylistic doctrine which may fairly be designated as the elaboration of the Theophrastean λόγος πρὸς τὰ πράγματα. Further it cannot be doubted that Peripatetic writers upon rhetoric, or rhetoricians under the influence of the Peripatetic school, must at an early time have made the logical connection between the λόγος πρὸς τὰ πράγματα and the corresponding chapter of the argument itself—the πίστεις ἐν αὐτῷ τῷ πράγματι. When this was once done rhetoric had forthwith defined for itself two styles corresponding to its two functions. But although the step was an inevitable one, and facilitated by the fact that the Stoics had shown what the characteristics and theory of such a pragmatic style would be, yet the actual record of this advance in rhetorical theory is not preserved.

But in the earliest treatise which we possess after the long break in our record, the incomplete work of the youthful Cicero, we find a tacit or implied recognition of two styles corresponding to the two aspects of the argument. The explicit definition of the matter was doubtless reserved for the portion *de elocutione* (I 27) which was never written. In II 47 it is explained that there are two kinds of arguments, the special ones upon which rest the proofs for the particular case in hand, and certain general ones which are chiefly serviceable for their emotional appeal to the auditor.[1] The kinds of loci communes are then enumerated and the passage concludes with the following distinction between the purposes of the two kinds of argument and the methods of their stylistic treatment: II 51 hi et ceteri loci omnes communes ex eisdem praeceptis sumuntur quibus ceterae argumentationes (i. e. the special ones); sed illae tenuius et subtilius et acutius tractantur: hi autem gravius et ornatius et cum verbis tum etiam sententiis excellentibus; in illis enim finis est ut id quod dicitur verum esse videatur: in his, tametsi hoc quoque videri oportet,

---

modum *fidem* faciat eis quibus volet persuadere, et quem ad modum *motum* eorum animis adferat. The analysis of the whole subject is referred to these two points of view throughout. So, for example, the parts of the oration in 4: quattuor (sunt partes orationis); earum duae valent ad rem *docendam*, narratio et confirmatio; ad *impellendos* animos duae, principium et peroratio.

[1] II 49 nam tum conceditur commune quiddam dicere cum diligenter aliqui proprius causae locus tractatus est, et auditoris animus aut renovatur ad ea quae restant, aut omnibus iam dictis exsuscitatur.

tamen finis est amplitudo.¹ Although the statement is made with reference to a particular subject and a particular class of arguments, yet it is clear that in the largest sense it summarizes the twofold aspects of rhetorical proof which we have thus far traced, the argument based upon the facts and looking to conviction and that which lies ἔξω τῶν πραγμάτων.² In this larger sense the matter is put in Part. Orat. 46: argumentandi autem duo genera sunt, quorum alterum ad fidem directo spectat, alterum se inflectit ad motum. Of these the first is the orderly dialectical process of setting forth premises and conclusions, the second looks to change and variety in the order of argument and, in the stylistic form, the use of every variety of figurative speech.³

More explicitly than in these examples the two modes of argument are used as the basis for the characterization of two oratorical styles in the well-known description of Galba and Laelius in Brutus 89: ex hac Rutilii narratione suspicari licet, cum duae summae sint in oratore laudes, una subtiliter disputandi ad docendum, altera graviter agendi ad animos audientium permovendos, multoque plus proficiat is qui inflammet iudicem quam ille qui doceat, elegantiam in Laelio, vim in Galba fuisse. The passage is an important one and I shall venture to tarry a moment in somewhat fuller explanation of it than has seemed necessary to the commentators on the text. Concerning the second of these summae in oratore laudes, nothing more need be said than the text affords: it is the emotional aspect of rhetoric, the ψυχαγωγία which Aristotle complained of as the only thing which the earlier theorists took into account. The first—*subtiliter disputare ad docendum*—is the pragmatic argumentation looking merely to intellectual conviction or persuasion, which Aristotle had introduced into rhetoric and defined as the most essential part of the subject. The editors, of course, compare the other passages of

[1] See Victorinus ad loc. Halm, R. L. M. p. 272. Cf. also II 49 omnia autem ornamenta elocutionis, in quibus et suavitatis et gravitatis plurimum consistit . . . . in communes locos conferuntur.

[2] Similarly two kinds of narrative are distinguished in forensic cases, I 27: unum genus est in quo ipsa causa et omnis ratio controversiae continetur; alterum, in quo digressio aliqua extra causam, aut criminationis aut similitudinis aut delectationis non alienae ab eo negotio quo de agitur aut amplificationis causa, interponitur.

[3] 47: est etiam illa varietas in argumentando et non iniucunda distinctio, ut cum interrogamus nosmet ipsos aut percontamur aut imperamus aut optamus, quae sunt cum aliis compluribus sententiarum ornamenta.

Cicero which define instruction (*docere*) as the first of the three *officia oratoris*. But they do not record the fact, significant for our inquiry, that this description is identical with the usual definitions of dialectic.

The Aristotelian division of logic into a higher and a lower type—apodeictic and dialectic—did not in any vital way survive the early Peripatetic school. And indeed there was perhaps good reason why it should not survive; since a distinction based upon the nature (the truth or untruth) of the premises is scarcely defensible. At all events the Stoics comprehended the whole method under their science of dialectic, and this became thenceforth the prevailing and universal conception. In Latin dialectical discourse is almost uniformly designated by *disputare* and its derivatives.[1] Its stylistic aspects are contemplated by Varro in his etymology of the word (L. L. VI 63): disputatio et computatio cum praepositione a putando,[2] quod valet purum facere.... sic is sermo in quo pure disponuntur verba, ne sit confusus atque ut diluceat, dicitur disputare. It is contrasted with the oratorical faculty *dicere* in Brutus 118, in characterization of the Stoic orators: omnes fere Stoici prudentissimi in disserendo sunt, et id arte faciunt suntque architecti paene verborum: eidem traducti *a disputando ad dicendum* inopes reperiuntur. Similarly in Orator 113: aliud videtur oratio esse aliud disputatio .... disputandi ratio et loquendi dialecticorum, oratorum dicendi et ornandi. But not only disputare (with its almost technical modifier *subtiliter*) but also *docere* itself points to identification of this function of oratory with dialectical proof. In the treatise de Ordine (I 1013, Migne) Augustine calls dialectic the disciplina disciplinarum, and proceeding, he says: haec docet docere, haec docet discere. With more exact applicability to our purpose Quintilian (XII 2, 11), in discussing the divisions of philosophy and beginning with the *pars dialectica*, demands that the orator shall possess it: quamquam ea non tam est minute atque concise in actionibus utendum quam in disputationibus, quia non *docere* modo, sed movere etiam ac delectare audientes debet orator. Similarly in the Preface 23 dialectic is designated simply as the *docendi ratio*. Finally, a word in regard to *elegantia*, with which the dialectical quality of Laelius' style is comprehended in con-

---

[1] Cf. Cicero passim. Quintilian ventures disputatrix = διαλεκτική, Augustine calls it the ars disputandi.

[2] The text as emended by Pomponius Laetus.

trast to the oratorical *vis* of Galba. It is a usage of the word well attested, though not sufficiently regarded, it would seem, by the lexicographers. But long ago Ernesti (Clavis Cic. s. v.) defined it correctly as subtilitas et acumen dialecticorum et philosophorum, and he cites the most noteworthy examples of this meaning. In argument it is keenness and subtlety, in style finished correctness of grammatical and idiomatic usage,[1] both of which meanings are here contemplated. The suggestion of ornament which the English word conveys is wholly lacking.

The two qualities exemplified by Galba and Laelius afford the starting point for a large number of the syncritical characterizations in the Brutus. Of these the most noteworthy is the juxtaposition of Cotta and Sulpicius in 201: quoniam ergo oratorum bonorum—hos enim quaerimus—duo genera sunt, unum attenuate presseque, alterum sublate ampleque dicentium. . . . inveniebat igitur acute Cotta, dicebat pure ac solute . . . . nihil erat in eius oratione nisi sincerum, nihil nisi siccum atque sanum.[2] . . fuit Sulpicius vel maxime omnium quos quidem ego audiverim grandis et, ut ita dicam, tragicus orator. In regard to the historical accuracy of this characterization it may be said that the description of Cotta's style corresponds to what we should expect from the considerations thus far presented concerning the origins of the plain style. We have derived this style from Theophrastus' definition of a λόγος πρὸς τὰ πράγματα which should be the linguistic instrument of philosophical discussion. Under the influence of Stoic teachers this style, as the complement of their dialectic, had gained a place in rhetoric. Its stylistic development had proceeded under the influence of Stoic grammatical and logical rules.[3] Now throughout Cicero's works Cotta appears as an enthusiastic devotee of philosophy. Furthermore (and this is of

---

[1] Cf. Auct. ad Heren. IV 17 elegantia est quae facit ut unum quidque pure et aperte dici videatur (cf. Varro's definition of *disputare* above) and Brutus 261 (of Caesar). *Elegantia* was the watchword of the Atticists and of the grammatical purists generally.

[2] In *acute* the logical acumen of his style is covered, in the remainder of the characterization its grammatical and idiomatic purity is emphasized, though in regard to these latter epithets it is to be said that their full significance will only appear from a review of the Stoic grammatical logical doctrines which culminated first in the Atticism of Cicero's time and two centuries later in the Archaism of Fronto.

[3] The further explanation of this point must be postponed to another occasion.

more significance) he was the nephew of the noble Rutilius Rufus whose Stoicism found expression not only in his acts but also in his oratorical style. It was in defense of his uncle that Cotta made his first public appearance as an orator, and we can imagine that loyalty to that *simplex ratio veritatis* (de Or. I 229), which characterized Rutilius' speech and did not suffice to save him against a corrupt and hostile court, was cherished by the nephew as an observance of piety. Sulpicius on the other hand is portrayed as wholly averse to philosophy and he repudiates its claims upon rhetoric even disdainfully.[1]

In similar contrast Crassus and Scaevola are placed in 145 ff. In Scaevola, the eminent jurisconsult, the qualities of precise and logical argument were especially conspicuous (qui quidem cum peracutus esset ad excogitandum quid in iure aut in aequo verum aut esset aut non esset), to which corresponded a style of singular brevity and suitableness to the matter (tum verbis erat ad rem cum summa brevitate mirabiliter aptus):[2] qua re fuit nobis orator in hoc interpretandi explanandi edisserendi genere mirabilis sic ut simile nihil viderim. The qualities looking to an effect outside of the argument itself he did not possess: in augendo in ornando in refellendo magis existimator metuendus quam admirandus orator. The characterization of the two orators in balanced antitheses which follows suggests to Brutus that a similar relation exists between Servius Sulpicius and Cicero, in which of course Servius is the counterpart of Scaevola and Cicero of Crassus. The style of Servius is not characterized in detail, but his superiority to Scaevola is attributed to his mastery of dialectic.[3]

It is noteworthy that in the Brutus, although the conventional three officia oratoris are defined (185), yet there appears no trace of the recognition of three corresponding styles. The oft repeated antitheses are the two which we have studied, though of course by no means all the orators are brought under this scheme of classification.

---

[1] De Or. III 146-7. He was a man of words, not of matter, Brutus 214.

[2] Cicero selects for mention two of the most characteristic of the five Stoic ἀρεταὶ λόγου—viz. συντομία (λέξις αὐτὰ τὰ ἀναγκαῖα περιέχουσα πρὸς δήλωσιν τοῦ πράγματος) and πρέπον (λέξις οἰκεία τῷ πράγματι = ad rem ... aptus), Diog. Laert. VII 59.

[3] Brutus 153: hic enim attulit hanc artem omnium artium maximam quasi lucem ad ea quae confuse ab aliis aut respondebantur aut agebantur.

We have now traced in such outlines as our record affords, the growth and gradual recognition of a twofold classification of style corresponding to the two aspects of proof, from its first suggestion by Aristotle to its formulation by Theophrastus, who, however, does not yet conceive of his λόγος πρὸς τὰ πράγματα as claiming a place in rhetoric. Under the growing influence of dialectical study and of its application to the practical affairs of daily life (in which the Stoics were the leaders) the rhetorical theorists took the step which neither Aristotle nor Theophrastus had taken, and assigned to its proper place in rhetoric the style of exact and pragmatic discussion, which had already been defined as appropriate for dialectic and philosophy. As the early Stoics admitted as legitimate no other form of argument except that based upon the facts of the case,[1] so in like manner they demanded that style confine itself to bare utility. But on the whole, the old pre-Aristotelian conception of rhetoric as an instrument of emotional transport continued naturally and inevitably to be the dominating one, though very considerable concessions were made to the demands of Aristotle for a more orderly system of argument, a point of view which was especially reinforced and reduced to practical rule by the Stoics. The result was that in practically all rhetorical teaching a place was granted, in theory at least, to exact and close argument, more or less touched by the science of dialectic (Hermagoras), and to a plain straightforward style suited to such ends. The common characteristics which all post-Aristotelian treatises show[2] go back thus to a synthesis of two influences, the purely rhetorical (especially Isocratean) and the philosophical (ultimately Aristotelian, immediately Stoic). Their combination belongs to a time considerably antecedent to the treatise de Inventione, which thus describes these two sources of influence: ex his duabus diversis sicuti familiis, quarum altera cum versaretur in philosophia non nullam rhetoricae quoque artis sibi curam adsumebat, altera vero omnis in dicendi erat studio et praeceptione occupata, unum quoddam est conflatum genus a posterioribus, qui ab utrisque ea quae commode dici videbantur in suas artes contulerunt (II 8, and see the sections preceding, 6 and 7).[3]

[1] Cf. Cic. de Or. I 229 (concerning Rutilius Rufus) and Quint. V preface init.
[2] Cf. note 3 on p. 260 above.
[3] Cf. also Quint. III 1, 14: hinc velut diversae secari coeperunt viae. . . . atque hinc vel studiosius philosophi quam rhetores, praecipueque Stoicorum ac Peripateticorum principes. The words which follow may perhaps be meant

The stylistic problem which we have thus far traced confirms the general truth of this passage, which might also be verified from other points of view.¹ For we have seen that the plain style is due to the demand, originating with the philosophers, for a more exact and logical system of argument, while the so-called grand style is rhetoric itself in the original conception of it as ψυχαγωγία.

As the *two* styles which we have thus far studied are the linguistic counterparts of the argument or proof conceived as twofold in character, so the *three* styles are referred to the threefold analysis of the officia oratoris—docere, conciliare (delectare), and movere. This relationship is expressly recognized by Cicero, who says (Or. 69): sed quot officia oratoris, tot sunt genera dicendi, subtile in probando, modicum in delectando, vehemens in flectendo, in quo uno vis omnis oratoris.² Whether Cicero here speaks with an historical consciousness of the common origin of the *genera dicendi* and the *officia oratoris* or not—for in rhetorical literature more than in most other subjects historical development was obscured by the dogmatic nature of instruction, with a consequent vagueness of historical consciousness—we may at any rate feel confident that this utterance represents the actual state of rhetorical theory in Cicero's time. That such was the case Quintilian also expressly attests (XII 10, 59): quorum (sc. tria genera dicendi) tamen ea fere ratio ('theory') est, ut primum docendi, secundum movendi etc. . . . praestare videatur officium. To the same point of view, Dionysius gives evidence in characterization of the style of Isocrates, which as containing elements of the plain and the embellished type of rhetoric he reckons to the middle style (λέξις μικτή): εἰς μὲν τὸ διδάξαι τὸν ἀκροατὴν σαφέστατα ὅ τι βούλοιτο, τὴν ἁπλῆν καὶ ἀκόσμητον ἑρμηνείαν ἐπιτηδεύει τὴν Λυσίου, εἰς δὲ τὸ καταπλήξασθαι . . . . τὴν ἐπίθετον καὶ κατεσκευασμένην φράσιν τῶν περὶ Γοργίαν ἐκμέμακται. Here may be added also the description of the styles which is preserved by Proclus (Photius, Bibliotheca 239): ὅτι τοῦ πλάσματος τὸ μέν ἐστιν ἰσχνόν, τὸ δὲ ἁδρόν, τὸ δὲ μέσον. καὶ τὸ

---

to indicate the synthesis of the two schools: facit deinde velut propriam Hermagoras viam, quam plurimi sunt secuti—but they are too vague to base definite inferences upon.

¹ Such as the combination of Aristotelian matter with the old Isocratean arrangement in such treatises as the Anonymus Seguerianus, or in the second half of Arist. Rhet. III; the doctrine of θέσις and ὑπόθεσις etc.

² The detailed application to the different parts of the oration is outlined in Orat. 124 ff.

μὲν ἁδρὸν ἐκπληκτικώτατόν ἐστι καὶ κατεσκευασμένον μάλιστα καὶ ποιητικὸν ἐπιφαῖνον κάλλος. τὸ δὲ ἰσχνὸν ... ἐξ ἀνειμένων¹ δὲ μᾶλλον συνήρτηται, ὅθεν ὡς ἐπίπαν τοῖς νοεροῖς² ἄριστά πως ἐφαρμόττει. The description has seemed worth quoting because, while it represents the developed doctrine of the three styles, it yet agrees so thoroughly with the Theophrastean division from which we started. For it is one of the few Greek descriptions in which the function of the χαρακτὴρ ἰσχνός is explicitly defined,—sc. τοῖς νοεροῖς, 'quae ratione intelleguntur'. These statements, therefore, of Cicero, Quintilian, Dionysius and Proclus are in exact agreement with our investigation to this point, which has derived the plain style from the λόγος πρὸς τὰ πράγματα.

The earliest occurrence of the threefold division is in the Auctor ad Herennium (IV 8, 11 ff.). And first, concerning the middle style, it will require no other investigation concerning its origin than to point out the inevitable rise of a *tertium quid* between the plain and the grand styles. As such the middle style is conceived of by this author,³ by Cicero in the three passages of the de Oratore where he touches on this division, and also in the Orator 21. The identification of the γένος ἀνθηρόν with the middle style⁴ is another matter and requires its own explanation.⁵ But to return to the Auctor ad Herennium. The theoretical relationship of the different styles to the parts of the oration is not expressly stated, but it is contained in numerous implications. In the first place, all three styles will be found present in all good oratory.⁶ The example of the grand style

---

¹ A term which plays a large rôle in divisions of style from the point of view of delivery and tone. Its antithesis is σύντονος. Cf. the anonymous scholia in Aphthonium, Walz II p. 3, 3, where the τρόποι ῥητορικῶν ἀναγνώσεων are analyzed. They correspond in some measure to the usual divisions of the styles—the τρόπος σύντονος to the grand style, the τρόπος ἀνειμένος to the plain style. The latter (ἀνειμένος) is described as διαλεκτικός τε καὶ διδασκαλικὸς καὶ συμβουλευτικός. Cf. the analysis of voice in Auct. ad Herenn. III 13, 23 into *sermo* and *contentio*, terms which have a large place in the literary criticism of Cicero. In de Officiis I 133 and II 48 they are the Latin names for the Stoic division of speech into διαλέγεσθαι and ἀγωνίζεσθαι.

² The correction of W. Schmid for γοεροῖς, Rh. Mus. 49, p. 134, 1.

³ IV 8, 11: mediocris est quae constat ex humiliore neque tamen ex infuma et pervulgatissima verborum dignitate. Cicero de Or. III 177, 199, 212.

⁴ Quintilian XII 10, 59; Cicero, Orator, 91 ff.

⁵ Proclus l. c. τὸ δὲ μέσον καὶ τοὔνομα μὲν δηλοῖ ὅτι μέσον ἐστὶν ἀμφοῖν. ἀνθηρὸν δὲ κατ' ἰδίαν οὐκ ἔστι πλάσμα, ἀλλὰ συνεκφέρεται καὶ συμμέμικται τοῖς εἰρημένοις.

⁶ IV 8, 11: sunt igitur tria genera . . . in quibus omnis oratio non vitiosa consumitur, and cf. 16 extr.

given is a peroration; it is highly figurative (rhetorical questions, exclamations), of elaborate stylistic finish, and almost wholly ἔξω τῶν πραγμάτων. The specimen of the middle style is a somewhat impassioned specimen of argumentation. It would seem to belong to the stage of the argument which the author in II 18, 28 calls the rationis confirmatio.[1] The example of the plain style is not, as we might have expected, a piece of objective and colorless argumentation, but a narratio. It is marked by an unconstrained conversational tone, corresponding to the characterization of this form as demissa ... usque ad usitatissimam puri consuetudinem sermonis. But while not argumentative it is still pragmatic and free from elaboration or emotional appeal; and it will be recalled that the narratio (p. above) is reckoned to the μέρος πραγματικόν. It should be kept in mind, further, that the two aspects of the plain style which may naturally be differentiated, a familiar conversational quality and argumentative cogency, are both contained in the Greek διαλέγεσθαι and its derivatives, and are both embraced in the Stoic principles of style which we have examined (συνήθεια). Thus διαλεκτική is not only for Plato, but even for the later Stoics the art of conversation.[2] Similarly, under the heading of delivery, in III 13, 23, sermo is divided into dignitas *demonstratio, narratio* and iocatio. It was therefore open to the writer to choose as a specimen of the figura attenuata either a narratio or a specimen of strict logical argument.[3] The object of this brief discussion of the three styles as they appear in the Auctor ad Herennium has been to show that they are thought of as corresponding to the parts of the oration and

---

[1] A complete and perfect argument is divided into five parts: propositio, ratio, rationis confirmatio, exornatio and complexio. The analysis is illustrated by examples. The ratio est quae causam demonstrat verum esse id quod intendimus brevi subiectione; that is the strict logical proof of the speaker's contention. The elaboration and amplification of this proof is the rationis confirmatio, of which the example of the figura mediocris seems to be meant as a specimen. This, then, is followed by the exornatio qua utimur rei honestandae et conlocupletandae causa confirmata argumentatione. The example of the exornatio is a highly elaborated piece of rhetoric comparable to the illustration of the figura gravis.

[2] Cf. Cic. de Off. I 133 and II 48 on the distinction between sermo and contentio. The former is dialectic, the latter is rhetoric. The discussion is drawn from Panaetius.

[3] On the examples of this style adduced by Cicero and Augustine see below, pp. 274, 277, 279.

its several functions: the figura gravis to the exornatio of the argument after it has already received logical demonstration (that is, τὰ ἔξω τῶν πραγμάτων), the figura mediocris to the elaboration of the simple demonstration, the figura attenuata to the narrative and the simple demonstration itself (αὐτὸ τὸ πρᾶγμα). By whom the intermediate stage of a middle style was defined it is of course impossible to say. We can only say that its origin as a natural intermediate step between the two characteristic forms is manifest, and that all three styles had been fixed and recognized for a considerable time anterior to this treatise.

From the subsequent history of the three styles I select a few aspects such as seem to me significant for the history and original meaning of the classification. But first of all I must justify myself for naming the Auctor ad Herennium as the first writer to present the doctrine of the three styles. For a curious and interesting example of the division, which might be reckoned as the earliest occurrence of it, is preserved for us by Gellius, who in turn draws from Varro. The account (Gellius VI 14) after presenting the conventional form of the doctrine, with the Greek and Latin terminology and with Latin examples, instances as illustrations the members of the embassy of Greek philosophers of the year 155: animadversa eadem tripertita varietas est in tribus philosophis, quos Athenienses Romam ad senatum legaverant. In the senate they spoke through the medium of an interpreter, but before this ipsi seorsum quisque ostentandi [ἐπιδείξεως] gratia magno conventu hominum dissertaverunt. Tum admirationi fuisse aiunt Rutilius et Polybius philosophorum trium sui cuiusque generis facundiam: 'Violenta' inquiunt 'et rapida Carneades dicebat, scita et teretia Critolaus, modesta Diogenes et sobria'. The matter is referred, it will be seen, to Rutilius and Polybius as sources, whose names, I think, must be understood in this way: that Rutilius in his memoirs, criticising (as elsewhere [1]) rhetorical ideals of public speaking from the standpoint of Stoicism and plain speech, illustrated the matter by an account of this famous embassy derived from a report of Polybius (whether written or oral), whose point of view would have been substantially the same as his own. As was to have been expected from the severe Stoicism which he represented, he condemns the style of Carneades as violenta et rapida (emotional and vehement), of Critolaus as clever and elaborated (scita et teretia), reserving praise only

[1] Cic. de Or. I 227 ff. Brutus 79 ff.

for Diogenes, the representative of Stoic sobriety and moderation of speech (modesta et sobria). As the names are arranged in Gellius (Carneades, Critolaus, Diogenes, corresponding, it would seem, to ἁδρόν ἰσχνόν μέσον) Carneades stands as the representative of the genus grande, Critolaus and Diogenes as the representatives of the genus subtile and medium respectively. But in Cicero de Or. II 157 ff., where the same embassy is described and the styles of the philosophers characterized, it must be inferred that Diogenes (as would naturally be expected) stands for the genus subtile and Critolaus for the genus medium.[1] The divergence of the two accounts indicates, as might be inferred from Gellius alone, that Rutilius did not have in mind the threefold analysis of style which we are considering, but merely contrasted the sober direct utterance of Diogenes with the rhetorical-emotional styles of Critolaus and Carneades. It was probably Varro who endeavored to adapt Rutilius' description to the current threefold scheme of stylistic theory.[2]

In point of time the three styles are found next in the de Oratore III 177, 199, 212. But in all three passages they are alluded to so briefly as to cast no light upon the author's conception of them or their history. It may be said, however, that the middle style is thought of merely as an intermediate stage between the other two. It is not until we come to the Orator that we find the characteristics of the three styles fully discussed, and here let us pause to note briefly the circumstances which condition Cicero's treatment of them.

The Orator, as has long been recognized, is not an abstract picture of the oratorical ideal, the crown of the edifice begun in the de Oratore and continued in the Brutus. For though Cicero apparently would have these treatises conceived of as a series, yet, in fact, it may confidently be affirmed that the Orator is a product of partisan debate, reaffirming with some few essential changes in point of view the general position of the de Oratore.[3]

[1] Cf. II 159 et genus sermonis adfert (Diogenes) non liquidum, non fusum ac profluens, sed exile, aridum, concisum atque minutum. 160 Critolaum ... puto plus huic nostro studio prodesse potuisse. 161 Carneadi vero vis incredibilis illa dicendi et varietas perquam esset optanda nobis.

[2] The possibility that Gellius in excerpting Varro's account has confused the positions of Critolaus and Diogenes may be suggested.

[3] The title *Orator* is, in fact, merely a variation of the earlier title *de Oratore*. In both the professed object is to delineate the ideal picture of the *orator*. Cf. de Or. I 118 sed quia de oratore quaerimus, *fingendus est nobis* oratione nostra

The germs of the conflict with opposing oratorical ideals, ideals which were entertained by most of the other eminent orators of Rome—Calvus, Brutus, Caesar, Asinius, Servius Sulpicius, Messala, Caelius and others—are discernible in many places of the de Oratore, but especially in III 38–53. Whether all these named are to be called Atticists or not it is certain that they stood for a more restrained and pragmatic type of oratory than that represented by Cicero and Hortensius. The theoretical and practical antitheses between exuberant and restrained rhetoric had been present in Rome for fully a century. Apart from the element which Roman character itself gave to these tendencies, they may be said to be derived mainly from the rhetoric of Asia Minor on the one hand, and from Stoical literary and grammatical theory on the other. Both schools are of nearly equal antiquity in Rome, but the influence of Stoicism can be traced more accurately and concretely. Crates, the Pergamene master and Stoic (168 B. C.), Diogenes of Babylon (155) and Panaetius (ca. 145) suffice to outline the chronology of this influence. Its theoretical position may be inferred from the general Stoic doctrine of style which we have cited above (and which seems to go back to Diogenes), and from the discussion of two types of utterance, *sermo* and *contentio*, which Cicero has drawn from Panaetius in de Officiis I 133 and II 48. It is, of course, what we should expect: advocacy of plain conversational speech as against the vehemence and emotional utterance of conventional rhetoric. This doctrine, received into the highest political and social circle of Rome, the younger Scipio, Laelius and their friends, became the starting point of a stylistic and oratorical ideal which we can trace through Lucilius, the Scaevolae, Rutilius Rufus, Q. Lutatius Catulus, Cotta, L. Macer (the father of Calvus) down to the Atticists and other contemporary opponents of Cicero.[1] But I anticipate a matter which to carry conviction demands a much

---

detractis omnibus vitiis *orator* atque omni laude cumulatus. See also I 202, and 264. Note also Or. 237 habes meum *de oratore* iudicium. The current conception, which Piderit especially has urged, that the three works represent an orderly sequence from the (1) theoretical foundations through the (2) historical exemplification to the (3) ideal picture, is purely fanciful.

[1] The sequence of the opposing school of emotional rhetoric is given by Cicero himself in his summary of Roman eloquence at the end of the Brutus (333): Galba, Lepidus, Carbo, Gracchi, Antonius, Crassus, [Cotta], Sulpicius, Hortensius, and the unnamed crown of it all—Cicero.

fuller treatment than can be here accorded to it. Let it suffice to have indicated in brief outline that the opponents whom Cicero combats are the bearers of a stylistic tradition which goes back to the Stoic influences (grammatical and philosophical) received by the Scipionic circle.

Now Cicero, defending himself against the suspicion of Asianism, is at pains in the Brutus to show that he had early seen the dangers and tastelessness of that manner and had deliberately abandoned it (313-16). Similarly in the Orator, while not abandoning his preference for the grand style, he is especially bent on showing that he has a definite and correct conception of the genus subtile, and in consequence he devotes to its description much more space than to either of the other styles. From his characterization some of the most essential elements may be noted. In soundness and penetration of argument it is supreme (acutae crebraeque sententiae ponentur et nescio unde ex abdito erutae, atque in hoc oratore dominabuntur 79); it does not aim at charm and lavishness of ornament (aberit... ornatum illud suave et adfluens 79); in composition it admits of negligence, as of one more concerned for the thought than the word (de re[1] hominis magis quam de verbis laborantis 77); its tone is conversational (summissus est et humilis, consuetudinem imitans 76). Cicero's characterization is careful and full. He is entirely in sympathy with the qualities which he describes, but not as embracing the whole equipment of the orator (quem [sc. subtilem] nisi quod solum ceteroqui recte quidam vocant Atticum 83). They fulfil but one of the functions of the orator and they fall short of that which is his highest and most characteristic trait, the power to sway and move—in quo uno vis omnis oratoris (69). The orator of the plain style accomplishes the end of instruction (docere) and reveals the qualities of the philosopher (ille summissus, quod acute et veteratorie dicit, sapiens iam 99), but the greater rewards are not his.

Sandys remarks on this passage that Cicero obviously has in mind Lysias as the type of the orator summissus. The suggestion doubtless rests on the fact that Dionysius names Lysias as the canon of this style. The matter admits neither of demonstration nor of certain refutation. But it may be questioned whether Cicero's characterization contemplates chiefly the ἀφέλεια

[1] Cf. the Theophrastean πρὸς τὰ πράγματα and the Stoic doctrine presented below p. 282.

—the simple lucidity and transparency of the Lysian or Xenophontean type. At any rate the example with which Cicero illustrates the style looks to pragmatic objectivity rather than to simplicity as its characteristic feature. Tota mihi causa pro Caecina de verbis interdicti fuit; res involutas definiendo explicavimus, ius civile laudavimus, verba ambigua distinximus (102). The qualities here described are chiefly dialectical, and in fact no one who reads the speech will call the style simple. Objective it is and pragmatic, but intricate and hard. The distinction is of some importance and it is not too much to say that Cicero's choice of illustration with his comment upon it, casts more light upon his understanding of the genus subtile than does his characterization. It is this quality of exact argumentation which is implied in the designation sapiens iam (cited above), since dialectic is the peculiar instrument of the philosopher, and it appears again in the technical dialectical words of description at the end of 99: qui enim nihil potest tranquille, nihil leniter, nihil *partite definite distincte* facete dicere, etc.

But the plain style, however admirable for its own ends, is in itself impotent to effect that ψυχαγωγία which is the true goal of oratorical effort. This can only be accomplished by the grand style which is in fact oratory itself. It was only this style which had won for eloquence place and historical significance in public life: hic est enim cuius ornatum dicendi et copiam admiratae gentes eloquentiam in civitatibus plurimum valere passae sunt (98). Because of this power it must, in any relative ranking of the styles, be placed first (at vero hic noster quem principem ponimus 99), a point of view to which Quintilian also bears evidence (XII 10, 63): quare si ex tribus his generibus necessario sit eligendum unum quis dubitet hoc praeferre omnibus: for it alone represents true oratorical power—haec est vere dicendi facultas (ib. 65). Its emotional power raises it above the necessity of objective argument—hoc dicente iudex . . . per omnes adfectus tractus huc atque illuc sequetur nec doceri desiderabit.[1]

It was this distinction between objective persuasion (fides) and the emotional effect which rises above persuasion and renders it

---

[1] Cf. περὶ ὕψους 1, 4 οὐ γὰρ εἰς πειθὼ τοὺς ἀκροωμένους ἀλλ' εἰς ἔκστασιν ἄγει τὰ ὑπερφυᾶ (sublimitas); and especially 15, 9 ἡ ῥητορικὴ φαντασία . . . κατακιρναμένη μέντοι ταῖς πραγματικαῖς ἐπιχειρήσεσιν οὐ πείθει τὸν ἀκροατὴν μόνον, ἀλλὰ καὶ δουλοῦται; also 15, 10 ἅμα γὰρ τῷ πραγματικῷ ἐπιχειρεῖν ὁ ῥήτωρ πεφάντασται, διὸ τὸν τοῦ πείθειν ὅρον ὑπερβέβηκεν τῷ λήμματι.

superfluous (motus)[1] which was the basis of Theophrastus' definition of the two types of λόγος: the one πρὸς τὰ πράγματα, ὑπὲρ ὧν ὁ λέγων πεῖσαι προτίθεται τοὺς ἀκροωμένους and the other πρὸς τοὺς ἀκροωμένους, which with all the resources of literary art seeks ἦσαί τε τὸν ἀκροατὴν καὶ ἐκπλῆξαι καὶ πρὸς τὴν πειθὼ χειρωθέντα ἔχειν.[2] The wide difference between these two styles Theophrastus indicates by putting the latter in the same category with poetry. Indeed the conception of true eloquence as a kind of poetry in prose was the very origin of the rhetorical style as Aristotle says,[3] and never ceased to be the accepted conception in circles uninfluenced by the rationalistic protest of some philosophical school. Abundant evidence on this point is available and has been put together by Norden.[4] It was from this point of view that Theophrastus (whom Quintilian quotes X 1, 27) said: plurimum oratori conferre lectionem poetarum, and the rhetorician adds truly: multique eius iudicium sequuntur. Cicero too bears evidence to his realization of the wide difference between this style and the others: sed multum interest inter hoc dicendi genus et superiora (Or. 98). From such considerations of the total difference between the pragmatic and the emotional styles there arose a doctrine of their irreconcilability, which has a curious antiquarian interest of its own, but which need here only be mentioned in illustration of the general principle of their fundamental divergence.[5]

[1] The terminology is drawn from Cic. Part. Oratoriae. Cf. πείθειν in the passages cited in the preceding note.

[2] Compare the phrase with the passage of περὶ ὕψους cited in note above. οὐ πείθει τὸν ἀκροατὴν μόνον ἀλλὰ καὶ δουλοῖται. Note also the similar contrast expressed in each by πράγματα, πραγματικός. For the whole text of the fragment of Theophrastus, see above p. 255.

[3] Rhet. III, 1 extr.

[4] Antike Kunstprosa I pp. 30 + 75 ff.

[5] The principal passages are these: Dionys. de Dem. 2 (of Thucydides and Lysias as the representatives of the two extremes of style) καθ' ὃ δὲ ἴσοι ἀλλήλων ἦσαν ἀτελεῖς. The point of view of Dionysius may be illustrated by comparison with de Isaeo 19 and 20 where the representatives of the two styles are grouped under the headings ποιητικοί and ἀκριβεῖς. More explicit is Demetrius (de Eloc. 36) who in defining four unmixed styles and their possible combinations says: μόνος δὲ ὁ μεγαλοπρεπὴς (χαρακτὴρ) τῷ ἰσχνῷ οὐ μίγνυται, ἀλλ' ὥσπερ ἀνθέστατον καὶ ἀντικείσθον ἐναντιωτάτω. For this reason therefore some had held that these are the only two fundamental styles, and that the rest are merely intervals between them. The point of view is refuted at some length by Hermogenes II 316 (Spengel) and perhaps also by Cicero de Or. III 175-177.

But although the conception of the plain style has its origin in the antithesis of pragmatic objective utterance to the language of emotional effect, yet it is by no means always true that the descriptions of the plain style reveal this conception. In fact some of the fullest do not, as for instance that of Demetrius de Eloc., who still bears evidence to the fundamental twofold division.[1] Instead of a plain style the χαρακτὴρ ἰσχνός becomes a style of simple elegance—a natural development enough when once the Atticists had begun to cast about for early examples of this style and found them in Lysias, Xenophon, Ctesias and others. Thenceforward in most of our sources the dominant characteristics recognized in it were formal and essentially rhetorical— ἀφέλεια, χάρις, etc.—rather than argumentative and dialectical. This can be seen most objectively perhaps in the rhetoric of Aristeides, the sophist of the second century, who defines two characters of style, the λόγος πολιτικός of which Demosthenes is the supreme type, and the λόγος ἀφελής which is illustrated chiefly from the Memorabilia of Xenophon.[2]

Without pausing to examine the evidence of numerous earlier writers which may be adduced for our purpose,[3] I would turn now to St. Augustine in whose works the conception of the plain style as the literary form of dialectical argument or proof appears with especial clearness; it is accompanied also by a theoretical doctrine of the distinction between this style and the language of emotional or sensuous appeal, which will be of service to us in understanding the development of the theory of the styles.

I shall call attention first to some passages of Augustine which distinguish in a stylistic way between dialectic and rhetoric. In the controversial treatise Contra Cresconium Donatistam (vol. IX. Migne coll. 445–6) we learn that Cresconius had warned his readers against the charm of Augustine's style and his rhetorical skill. Augustine replies with the Stoic conception of eloquence: facultas dicendi est, congruenter explicans quae sentimus; qua

---

[1] See passage cited in note 5 p. 275.
[2] The matter demands however fuller investigation.
[3] But note Tacitus Dial. 31: sunt apud quos adstrictum et collectum singula statim argumenta concludens dicendi genus plus fidei meretur: apud hos dedisse operam dialecticae proficiet. See also the interesting polemical utterances of Quintilian in V 14, 27–33, directed against a school which in the treatment of the argument was dialectical (27 and 32), and affected the manner of the ancients; in style plain and direct (33).

tunc utendum est cum recta sentimus. It is good or bad according to the nature of its utterances, not in itself (1, 2). Cresconius himself has shown by his own eloquence in assailing eloquence that his attack on this point is contentious rather than sincere (2, 3). Similarly in regard to dialectic Cresconius has sought to prejudice his followers by warning them to beware of Augustine's skill, as if it were some pagan trick incongruous with the Christian character (13, 16). But in fact what is dialectic except skilful argumentation (peritia disputandi); and indeed just such art as Cresconius himself is using against Augustine: inspicio sermonem tuum, istum ipsum quem ad me scripsisti; video te quaedam copiose ornateque explicare, hoc est eloquenter: quaedam vero subtiliter arguteque disserere hoc est dialectice. Cresconius has sought to impose on the ignorance of his audience by inveighing against rhetoric and dialectic, both of which he thus employs in a false and sophistical way (14, 17 extr.).

The true dialectician uses the art for the necessary purpose of distinguishing between the true and the false (15, 19), and of this art, as of true eloquence, the Holy Scriptures afford abundant examples (14, 18).[1] Hoc ille verus disputator si late diffuseque faciat, eloquenter facit, alioque tunc censetur augeturque vocabulo, ut dictor potius quam disputator vocetur; sicut illum locum Apostolus copiose dilatat atque diffundit (16, 20): 'in omnibus' inquit (II Cor. 6, 4-10) 'commendantes nosmetipsos ut Dei ministros, in multa patientia, in tribulationibus, in angustiis, in plagis, in carceribus,' etc.—a passage of such resonant and triumphant rhetoric in the Latin version which Augustine uses that it is hard to refrain from citing it in full. Upon this he comments: quid enim hoc stilo apostolico uberius et ornatius, id est eloquentius, facile invenis?

Turning then to examples of dialectic he continues: si autem presse atque constricte, magis eum disputatorem quam dictorem appellare consueverunt: qualiter agit idem Apostolus de circumcisione et praeputio patris Abraham, vel distinctione legis et gratiae.

My purpose in setting forth this discussion has been to show as nearly as possible by concrete examples Augustine's conception of the practical distinction between dialectic and rhetoric.

[1] Augustine demonstrates the presence of dialectic in the Scriptures by citing passages in which the word *disputare* occurs; the argument is captious, but interesting as revealing the technical character of the word.

Some passages of the treatise of Cresconius were rhetoric (eloquentia), others were dialectic. Examples from Cresconius he does not give (and we can well enough spare them), but the superb specimen of St. Paul's eloquence, contrasted with the close objective argumentation of the other passages of Scripture which are designated as dialectic, makes it clear that from a linguistic point of view the distinction between the two forms of presentation is a distinction between two types of literary style. The theoretical principle of differentiation as explained by Augustine himself we shall examine presently.

The treatise De Doctrina Christiana deals with the method of interpretation and exposition of Christian doctrine.[1] It is a work of much interest for the personality of Augustine as well as for the history of Christian rhetoric, and deserves more thorough and historical interpretation than it has received.[2] The fourth book, which deals with the question of presentation or style, is perhaps of most general interest. A portion of it I shall here take up in which the doctrine of the three styles is applied to Christian eloquence.

In book II 41 (I cite by the smaller divisions of Migne) Augustine has reviewed briefly the value of the various disciplines for the Christian teacher. After a rather full discussion of dialectic (48–53), he turns briefly to rhetoric in 54: sunt etiam quaedam praecepta uberioris disputationis, quae iam eloquentia nominatur. To these two arts the duty of the Christian orator corresponds (IV 6). If his auditors require instruction, by narrative or argument the necessary facts and conclusions are to be placed before them; but if they require that the knowledge which they already have shall be transmuted into action (moveri), then there is need of eloquence (maioribus dicendi viribus opus est[3].) The underlying distinction here is, it will be seen, the distinction between dialectic and rhetoric, and in the paragraphs which follow (7 and 8) the adverbs *sapienter* and *eloquenter* continue the same antithesis.

[1] I 1: duae sunt res quibus nititur omnis tractatio Scripturarum: modus inveniendi quae intelligenda sunt (= books I–III) et modus proferendi quae intellecta sunt (= book IV).

[2] The treatises of Ferd. Colincamp, La Méthode Oratoire dans St. Augustine (Diss. Paris 1848), and of A. Lezat, De Oratore Christiano apud St. Aug. (ib. 1871), are serviceable for a general introduction to the subject.

[3] Ibid. extr. Ibi observationes et increpationes, concitationes et coercitiones et quaecumque alia valent ad commovendos animos sunt necessaria.

Without following further the intervening argument, I pass now to 27, which introduces the three Ciceronian officia oratoris. Dixit ergo quidam eloquens et verum dixit ita dicere debere eloquentem ut doceat ut delectet ut flectat. The relationship of these three functions is defined with reference to the distinction drawn in II 55 between dialectic and rhetoric: horum trium quod primo loco positum est, hoc est docendi necessitas, in *rebus* est constituta quas dicimus; reliqua duo, in *modo* quo dicimus.[1] That is, of the three functions of the orator, *docere* falls in the province of the dialectician, *delectare* and *movere* of the rhetorician. The first per se may wholly disregard form if only the speaker conveys his thought to the mind of another (si vero intellectus est, quocumque modo dixerit, dixit). But the auditor is not always patient to listen, nor, though he knows the truth, is he always moved to carry it into effect: sicut est autem ut teneatur ad audiendum delectandus auditor, ita flectendus ut moveatur ad agendum (27 extr.).

To these three functions correspond the three styles, the relation of which to the officia oratoris is described in words adapted from Cicero (34 extr.): is erit eloquens qui ut doceat poterit parva submisse, ut delectet modica temperate, ut flectat magna grauditer dicere. In explanation of the words *parva submisse* Augustine digresses (35) to point out that the Christian preacher has always to do with great subject-matter, lest the words of Cicero should mislead; but though his theme is always great, yet it must not always be treated in the grand style: for where there is need of *instruction*, even in great matters, the style should be plain and subdued (38 init.). For example, the explanation of the unity of the Trinity requires careful discussion (disputatione) in order that a difficult subject may be apprehended as clearly as possible: here is no place for the ornaments of style, but only for explanation and demonstration (38).

In 39 Augustine passes over to a more detailed characterization of the three styles on the basis of examples chosen from Holy Scripture. The *dictio submissa* is first illustrated with passages drawn from the third and fourth chapters of Paul to the Galatians. They are typical specimens of the close logical manner of St. Paul, exactly similar to the kind of discussions which Augustine said in his reply to Cresconius show the presence of dialectic in

---

[1] See the formulation of this distinction in the de Dialectica, p. 283 below.

the sacred writings (see above p. 277). The characteristics of the examples chosen are explained by intercalated observations. The first is more narrative and didactic, the second argumentative, and as it proceeds it clears the ground by the anticipation of objections or difficulties which might occur to the reader. The strict dialectical character of the style is commented on as follows: pertinet ergo ad docendi curam non solum aperire clausa et nodos solvere quaestionum, sed etiam dum hoc agitur, aliis quaestionibus, quae fortassis inciderint, ne id quod dicimus improbetur per illas aut refellatur, occurrere.

It will be seen from the examples cited and from the characterizing words of Augustine that the dictio submissa is scarcely what we should call a simple style (λόγος ἀφελής), nor would it, I think, occur to the modern reader to instance passages of close reasoning in Paul's Epistles as examples of such a style. One might have looked more naturally for some simple narrative from the Gospels. But in fact not only here, but also in the specimens given from Cyprian and Ambrosius the characteristic traits are argumentative and are designated as such.[1] Indeed this style is conceived of by Augustine as the instrument for the most involved and intricate discussion (39 extr.): fit autem ut cum incidentes quaestioni aliae quaestiones, et aliae rursus incidentibus incidentes pertractantur atque solvuntur, in eam longitudinem ratiocinationis extendatur intentio, ut nisi memoria plurimum valeat atque vigeat, ad caput unde agebatur disputator redire non possit. It is in short, as the examples and the words of characterization show (quaestio, ratiocinatio, disputator), dialectic itself looked at from the linguistic side or, in other words, conceived of as style. The description of Augustine contains not a few allusions to or reminiscences of Cicero's treatment of the same style in the Orator. In general however the dialectical character of the style, which we found implied in some of Cicero's terms and especially in his choice of an example (his oration pro Caecina), is more strongly emphasized.[2]

[1] Cf. 45 (On a passage from Cyprian): iam solvere incipiens propositam quaestionem. 44 (Ambrosius de Spiritu Sancto): res suscepta . . . rerum documenta desiderat.

[2] This may be seen very well by comparison of the following passages, Orator 79: acutae crebraeque sententiae ponentur et nescio unde ex abdito erutae; and Augustine 56: plerumque autem dictio ipsa submissa, dum solvit difficillimas quaestiones et inopinata manifestatione demonstrat, dum *sententias acutissimas de nescio quibus quasi cavernis, unde non sperabatur*, eruit et ostendit.

In contrast to the genus summissum stand the other two styles, the genus medium and the genus grande, corresponding to the contrasted functions of the orator: (1) docere and (2) delectare and movere. The first of these has to do with the matter of eloquence, the other two with the manner (above p. 279). As the plain style is thought of as the stylistic aspect of dialectic, so the other two styles are in reality but two aspects or phases of rhetoric looked at from the standpoint of style. For rhetoric is fundamentally conceived of as the art of effecting an emotional transport (ψυχαγωγία) [1] which shall take the place of intellectual persuasion. Its ends may be accomplished roughly speaking in either of two ways: (1) by language relying for effect chiefly upon the vivid and emotional conception of the thought (σχήματα τῆς διανοίας), or (2) by the more subtle and sensuous elements of sound and rhythm σχήματα τῆς λέξεως.[2] In a rough way Demosthenes may be instanced as an example of the former type, Isocrates of the latter. With the first of these methods the grand style is identified (movere), with the second the middle (delectare). Like Cicero, Augustine attaches most importance to the grand style, which together with the plain style affords the Christian orator his essential instruments. These two styles and recognition of their aim (quod efficere intendunt) are especially necessary for those qui sapienter et eloquenter volunt dicere. Examples of the grand style, well chosen and effective, from the Epistles of Paul are presented in 42, of which the first (II Cor. 6, 2-11) is the same as was adduced in the polemic against Cresconius to show the presence of rhetoric in the sacred writings. As in the treatise De Dialectica, to which we shall presently turn, the demand is made that the dialectician shall lend color and grace to disputation by rhetorical means, and that on the other hand the rhetorician shall use the bones and sinews of dialectic for the framework of his utterances, so in each of the three styles Augustine demands that some qualities of the other two shall be

---

[1] Plato Phaedrus 271 D: ἐπειδὴ λόγου δύναμις τυγχάνει ψυχαγωγία οὖσα. Cf. the interesting paper of Hirzel, Über das Rhetorische und seine Bedeutung bei Plato, Leipzig, 1871.

[2] The relation of these two methods to each other is well defined in 42: grande autem dicendi genus hoc maxime distat ab isto genere temperato, quod non tam verborum ornatibus comptum est, quam violentum animi affectibus. Nam capit etiam illa ornamenta paene omnia; sed ea si non habuerit, non requirit.

present. The genus submissum for instance shall not only be listened to with understanding (intelligenter), but also with pleasure (libenter), and with persuasion which shall lead to action (oboedienter); nolumus enim fastidiri etiam quod submisse dicimus; ac per hoc volumus non solum intelligenter, verum etiam libenter audiri (56). Enough has been presented to show that Augustine conceives of the genus submissum as the stylistic aspect of dialectic, the genus medium and the genus grande as two stylistic aspects of rhetoric.

But before leaving Augustine I would call attention to a portion of the treatise De Dialectica, in which is contained an explicit theory of the stylistic differences between dialectic and rhetoric, essentially identical with the relation which we have found to exist between the genus submissum and the two other styles as presented by Augustine. It harks back to the distinction between the λόγος πρὸς τὰ πράγματα and the λόγος πρὸς τοὺς ἀκροωμένους of Theophrastus from which we started, and is, in fact, I believe, merely a Stoic development and systematization of that doctrine.

The ultimate differences are derived from the fundamental *vis verborum* (ch. VII):[1] vis verbi est qua cognoscitur quantum valeat. valet autem tantum quantum movere audientem potest. Porro movet audientem

aut secundum se
aut secundum id quod significat
aut ex utroque communiter.

I. The first division touches the sensuous or non-intellectual aspects of the word: sed cum secundum se movet

aut ad solum sensum pertinet
aut ad artem
aut ad utrumque.

Of these three divisions the first again receives a twofold subdivision: (1) sensus aut *natura* movetur aut *consuetudine*. (a) *Natura*—as when the ear is offended by the harshness of sound in 'Artaxerxes', or is soothed (mulcetur) by the liquid softness of

[1] The treatise was relegated to the *spuria* by the Benedictines, whom Migne follows, placing it in the appendix to vol. I and rendering it often quite unintelligible by careless printing. It is carefully edited and elucidated with valuable parallels by W. Crecelius, Elberfeld, 1857 (Program of the Gymnasium). It is perhaps best preserved in the famous codex Bernensis no. 363 and is therefore now accessible in the splendid Leyden series of photographic facsimiles.

'Euryalus'. (b) *Consuetudine*—as when the ear is offended or pleased by words which habit or convention has rendered disagreeable or pleasing. (2) The division *ad artem* is not perfectly clear, but it seems to cover the recognition of the grammatical form of the word, its rhythmical (metrical) value, or whatever else concerning words is taught *in arte*: it does not include the meaning or intellectual content of the word.

II. The second main division, *secundum id quod significat* looks purely to the meaning of words, without reference to the sensuous, associative, or emotional effect which they may derive from any of the preceding considerations: iam vero non secundum se sed secundum id quod significat verbum movet quando per aurem accepto signo animus nihil aliud quam rem ipsam intuetur, cuius illud signum est quod accepit: ut cum Augustino nominato nihil aliud quam ego ipse cogitor ab eo cui notus sum, vel qui alium novit qui Augustinus vocetur.

III. Both effects may be produced at once (ex utroque communiter): tunc et ipsa enuntiatio (= secundum se) et id quod ab ea enuntiatur (= secundum id quod significat) simul advertitur.

From this twofold nature of words are derived two aspects of language as a whole, the one looking purely to the expression of thought or meaning (*enuntiatum*), the other to an extra-intellectual effect of sensuous, associative, or emotional character dependent upon the form of expression itself (*enuntiatio*). The two points of view are designated as the characteristic (not exclusive) aspects of dialectic and rhetoric respectively: cum igitur tantam vim tamque multiplicem appareat esse verborum, quam breviter pro tempore summatimque attigimus, duplex hinc consideratio [sensus] nascitur: partim propter explicandam veritatem, partim propter conservandum decorem; quorum primum ad dialecticum, secundum ad oratorem maxime pertinet. The features of language thus defined are unfortunately too often separated: quamvis enim nec disputationem deceat ineptam nec eloquentiam oporteat esse mendacem, tamen et in illa [sc. dialectica] saepe atque adeo paene semper audiendi delicias discendi cupido contemnit, et in hac [sc. eloquentia] imperitior multitudo quod ornate dicitur etiam vere dici arbitratur. The ideal is for each to borrow something from the characteristic (*proprium*) domain of the other: the two should be inseparably associated as are the bones and muscles (dialectic) in relation to the external beauty (rhetoric) of the human form: ergo cum appareat quid sit uniuscuiusque proprium, manifestum est et disputatorem, si qua ei delectandi cura est rhetorico colore aspergendum et oratorem, si veritatem persuadere vult, dialecticis quasi nervis atque ossibus esse roborandum, quae ipsa natura in corporibus nostris nec firmitati virium subtrahere potuit nec oculorum offensioni patere permisit.[1]

The interest and importance of this chapter of Augustine for our inquiry is not slight; for whatever may be thought to-day of its ultimate worth, it affords us a more sharply defined and explicit theory of the distinction of styles than is elsewhere to my knowledge preserved. It is the theory upon which his presentation of the three styles in the De Doctrina Christiana is based. For there the styles correspond to the officia oratoris; and of these the first—*docere*, in rebus est constitutum quas dicimus: the other two in modo quo dicimus (IV 27), a distinction identical with that drawn between the *content* of language (*enuntiatum*) and the *form* in which this is contained (*ipsa enuntiatio*).

It need scarcely be said that this analysis is not original with Augustine, but goes back to the source from which the whole treatise is drawn. That this source is Stoic and, at latest, contemporary with Varro, is certain.[2] But this Stoic source does not represent the actual origin of the ideas here advanced, but drew in turn from earlier Peripatetic speculations concerning the relation of language to thought and the consequent fundamental divisions of style. For the distinction here made between the vis verbi secundum se[3] and secundum id quod significat is essentially no more than an abstract and scholastic version (looking to more universal applicability) of the Theophrastean doctrine of

---

[1] Cf. Quintilian, Prooem. 24 (referring to dialectic—ratio docendi): nam plerumque nudae illae artes nimiae subtilitatis adfectatione frangunt atque concidunt quidquid est in oratione generosius et omnem sucum ingenii bibunt et ossa detegunt: quae ut esse adstringi nervis suis debent, sic corpore operienda sunt.

[2] Varro is recognized as the probable source of the treatise by Wilmanns, de Varronis lib. gram. pp. 16-19. Reitzenstein, M. Ter. Varro (Leipz., 1901) p. 75, seeks to show that the treatise is an excerpt from De Lingua Latina I. Cf. also R. Schmidt, Gram. Stoicorum p. 26 ff., and Sandys, Hist. of Cl. Scholarship, p. 224, note 1. For some earlier allusions to the general doctrine see note, p. 285.

[3] It need scarcely be said the doctrine is not confined to the single word, but extends to the whole artistic structure of language—figures, rhythm, periodicity, etc.

the λόγος πρὸς τοὺς ἀκροωμένους and the λόγος πρὸς τὰ πράγματα, from which we started.

We have seen that in Augustine's account the value of the word or form of speech *secundum se* is something independent of or superinduced upon the meaning or intellectual content itself; something which from its sensuous (*natura*) or associative (*consuetudine*) significance we may call in a general way its emotional power. It is from the same point of view that Theophrastus defines the nature of the λόγος πρὸς τοὺς ἀκροωμένους. For in the same way it takes into account only as one of two considerations the actual meaning conveyed to the listeners, οἷς καὶ σημαίνει τι. Its primary function and characteristic is to select words which shall be more impressive and beautiful (σεμνότερα) than the proper or common (κοινὰ καὶ δεδημευμένα) ones with which the thought itself might be most accurately expressed;[1] to weave these into such harmonious combinations (καὶ ταῦτα ἐναρμονίως συμπλέκειν) as to delight and sway the listener (ἧσαι καὶ ἐκπλῆξαι), who is thus overmastered and does not demand intellectual persuasion (πρὸς τὴν πειθὼ χειρωθέντα [τὸν ἀκροατὴν] ἔχειν).[2]

The λόγος πρὸς τὰ πράγματα on the other hand corresponds exactly to the doctrine set forth under the caption *secundum id quod significat*. Both points of view contemplate a use of language merely as a medium for the communication of thought (πράγματα, res): secundum id quod significat verbum movet quando per aurem accepto signo animus nihil aliud quam rem ipsam (αὐτὸ τὸ πρᾶγμα) intuetur, cuius illud signum est quod accepit.[3] As in Augustine this function of language is employed

---

[1] Cf. Arist. Poetics, 22 init. cited p. 254.

[2] Cf. Augustine's similar comment, with the Stoic reprobation of such effect (l. c. 8 extr.): imperitior multitudo quod ornate dicitur etiam vere dici arbitratur. The Theophrastean designation πρὸς τοὺς ἀκροωμένους is suggested by Augustine's words *audiendi delicias* referring to the language of rhetoric, and by the constant appeal to the ear in the division *secundum se*.

[3] The same point of view is contained in Quintilian VIII 2, 6: proprietas non ad nomen sed ad vim significandi refertur, nec *auditu* sed *intellectu* perpendenda est, with which compare especially Cic. de Or. III 150. Cf. Orat. 80: probatur in propriis usitatisque verbis quod aut *optime sonat* aut *rem maxime explanat*. There are many passages of this kind which call for more careful collection and comparison. Cf. Part. Orat. 17, and Quint. VIII 3, 16 ff. It is against such a background of more or less elaborate theory that the *res* of philosophy are contrasted with the *verba* of rhetoric (and grammar). Cic. Orat. 51: quod si in philosophia tantum interest quem ad modum dicas, ubi *res spectatur*, non *verba penduntur*, etc. Cf. Aristeides (Spg. II 500, 27): ὅταν

propter explicandam veritatem and is therefore the peculiar instrument of the dialectician, so in Theophrastus the division πρὸς τὰ πράγματα will be the special concern of the philosopher (ὁ φιλόσοφος προηγουμένως ἐπιμελήσεται) refuting the false and setting forth the true (τό τε ψεῦδος διελέγχων καὶ τὸ ἀληθὲς ἀποδεικνύς).

The identification of the style of elaborate and florid embellishment with the genus medium is one of the earliest distortions of this fundamental theory. It was recognized in antiquity as a distortion, and criticised in the words of Proclus cited above (p. 286, n. 5). Dismissing for the moment consideration of the reasons for this identification, let us note (as was suggested above p. 281) that in reality this conception of the genus medium is merely as one type of rhetorical style, co-ordinate with the emotional form which more and more usurped the designation of the grand style. The florid and embellished style is in no essential sense an intermediate stage between the other two, and indeed in stylistic elaboration it is furthest removed from the plain style. It is the Gorgianic rhetoric as developed by Isocrates and his school. Demetrius of Phaleron is Cicero's example of the type, and its *provenance* in general is correctly indicated by him in Orator 96: hoc totum e sophistarum fontibus defluxit in forum.[1] The anomaly of its designation as a middle style he suggests in the same place: spretum a subtilibus, repulsum a gravibus, in ea de qua loquor mediocritate consedit—that is, as one may infer, it took the only place that was left. In Cicero's theory this analysis of the rhetorical style into two forms corresponds to the two officia oratoris which he designates in the Orator as *delectare* and *movere*. As *docere* is the philosophical or dialectical feature of the orator's art (docendi necessitas in *rebus* est constituta) so the other two are its characteristically rhetorical aspects (reliqua duo in *modo* quo dicimus).[2] Both were contemplated in Theophrastus' λόγος πρὸς τοὺς ἀκροωμένους the function of which was to please

---

τις μὴ φιλοτιμῆται πρὸς τὴν λέξιν, ἀλλὰ καὶ πρὸς τὰ πράγματα ἀποβλέπῃ. See also Seneca Epp. 100, 10 and 11, and especially Quint. VIII 3, 11-13 for the range of the *vis verbi secundum se*. For this latter phrase cf. Ammonius In Arist. de Interp. p. 65, 5 (Busse): οἱ τούτων (sc. ῥητορική and ποιητική) ἑκατέραν ἐπιτηδεύοντες περί τε τοὺς λόγους αὐτοὺς καθ' αὑτοὺς ἔχουσι, ῥήτορες μὲν τοὺς ῥυθμοὺς αὐτῶν καὶ τὰς περιόδους καὶ τὰ σχήματα πολυπραγμονοῦντες, γραμματικοὶ δέ κτλ.

[1] With this compare the descriptions of the style of the sophists in Orat. 38 and 65.
[2] Aug. de Doctr. Chr. IV 27.

(ἦσαι) and to move (καταπλήξασθαι). The point of view is of the widest diffusion in ancient theory, but brief illustration of it will not perhaps be superfluous.

The elements are perhaps nowhere so sharply defined positively as they are indicated negatively in a definition of the stylistic error κακοζηλία, which Diomedes (451, 10) preserves: haec fit aut nimio *cultu* aut nimio *tumore*, a scheme of analysis which corresponds exactly to Cicero's division of the Asiatic rhetoric into two types (Brutus 325): unum sententiosum et argutum, sententiis non tam gravibus et severis quam concinnis et venustis. Aliud ... non tam sententiis frequentatum quam verbis volucre atque incitatum (and a little later—sententiarum venustas and orationis cursus). Both make appeal to the emotions in the widest sense, the one primarily by ornateness of stylistic form (cultus), the other by vehemence and passion of conception and utterance (tumor, vis).[1]

Both types reach far back into the history of rhetoric and in fact, perhaps, stand side by side at the very beginning of it, in the persons of Gorgias and Thrasymachus, if we may extricate the latter from the ill-fated association with Gorgias which is common in most of our later sources.[2] But the theoretical differentiation of the two rhetorical styles thus represented belongs apparently to a time subsequent to Theophrastus, when the fame of Demosthenes was beginning to encroach upon the long supremacy of Isocrates. It may have been suggested by the Aristotelian distinction between the λέξις γραφική and ἀγωνιστική as defined in Rhet. III 12. In such case the λέξις γραφική came early to be almost synonymous with λέξις ἐπιδεικτική (embracing history), which as Aristotle had said was γραφικωτάτη.[3] But it seems to me more likely that it depends upon some theoretical division such as is hinted at in the fragment of Theophrastus.[4] But however

---

[1] Cf. Augustine de Doctr. Chr. IV 42: grande autem dicendi genus hoc maxime distat ab isto genere temperato, quod non tam verborum ornatibus comptum est, quam violentum animi affectibus. Nam capit etiam illa ornamenta paene omnia, sed ea si non habuerit non requirit.

[2] This interpretation of Thrasymachus is based upon Plato, Phaedrus 267 C and is developed by Schwartz, De Thrasymacho Chalcedonio, Progr. Rostock, 1892.

[3] In de Or. II 94 the pupils of Isocrates are partim in pompa (ἐπιδεικτικοί) partim in acie (ἀγωνιστικοί) inlustres. The same ones in Or. 40 are partim in scribendo partim in dicendo principes.

[4] One is tempted to put in this connection the two goals of literary art which Dionysius defines in de Comp. 10, ἥ τε ἡδονὴ καὶ τὸ καλόν, making them the

we explain the origins of this distinction it is certain that at a later time the doctrine of the figures contributed most to the sharpness of definition of the two types: the σχήματα λέξεως characterizing the genus floridum, the σχήματα διανοίας the genus grande.[1] For the designation of the genus floridum as a middle style I have been able to find no cogent reason, unless it be with reference to delivery, where the smooth and relaxed (ἀνειμένος) tone might seem to place this style nearer to the conversational manner of the pragmatic style than to the vigor and tenseness (σύντονος) of the genus grande.

Concerning the Greek names for the stylistic characters, ἰσχνός and ἁδρός, which seem to be the most fixed and constant designations amidst a large variety of other terms, they are of course metaphors drawn from the human form. From the normal standpoint of Greek artistic feeling, as well as from the actual usage of the words, it would seem probable that ἰσχνός was originally a term of reproach or contempt set over against ἁδρός with its implication of praise or admiration. One might conjecture, in short, that ἰσχνός (λόγος) was originally the contemptuous designation with which the rhetorician spoke of the dry and meagre language of his rival the philosopher. It is at any rate true that the reproaches which the rhetoricians direct against the language of philosophy are of this character (sermo tenuis, exsanguis, exilis, aridus, etc.). Accordingly, Dialectica in Martianus Capella is pallidior (328) femina contractioris corporis

---

criterion for determination of the two forms of composition, the σύνθεσις γλαφυρά and αὐστηρά. The analysis of the qualities belonging to ἡδονή (ch. 11) reveals essentially the qualities of the middle style conceived of as a genus floridum; the qualities assigned to τὸ καλόν (ib.) are those which belong rather to the grand style—μεγαλοπρέπεια, βάρος, σεμνολογία, ἀξίωμα—though in the nature of things in a treatise de compositione the purely stylistic aspects of the matter predominate over the emotional features of the style. It is certain, however, that there is a relationship between Dionysius' two types of composition and the two forms of the grand style which are defined by Fortunatianus (R. L. M. p. 126): ἁδρὸν uniforme est? non; nam est aut αὐστηρὸν aut ἀνθηρόν. It is the same analysis which Cicero gives in Orator 20, dividing the grand style into two forms: (1) alii aspera tristi horrida oratione, (2) alii levi et structa et terminata.

[1] Cf. Cic. Or. 95: in idem (medium) genus orationis verborum cadunt lumina omnia, multa etiam sententiarum. The latter, however, belong essentially to the style of vehemence, and to their skilful use was attributed the superiority of Demosthenes (Or. 136 and Brutus 141).

(329), in contrast to Rhetorica, who is sublimissimi corporis (426), opimi oris (337).

There are of course many other special problems connected with our subject which call for explanation. But the limits of space here available forbid further discussion. The origin of the related faults of style ($παρεκβάσεις$)[1] I have explained in an earlier study by reference of them to the Peripatetic conception of the excess in relation to the mean of style. It was applied first only to language of rhetorical elaboration ($λόγος\ πρὸς\ τοὺς\ ἀκροωμένους$), and the transgression of the mean in the direction of excess is designated by Aristotle and Theophrastus as $τὸ\ ψυχρόν,\ ψυχρότης$. After the recognition of the plain and the middle (or other) styles it was transferred to them also.

The prevailing ideas concerning the characters are derived from Dionysius, who makes the middle style the most admirable. The point of view has seemed a natural Peripatetic one, in view of which the general designation in our other sources (Cicero, Quintilian, Demetrius, Ps.-Longinus, Augustine) of the grand style as pre-eminent has seemed remarkable and distorted. The difficulty, however, disappears when it becomes clear that our styles (whether three or more) represent a fundamental two-fold analysis, so that the pre-eminence awarded to the grand style is merely recognition of its original character as artistic prose, in contrast to language purely as a vehicle of thought.

The development of the idea of ornament in the plain style is perhaps the most important problem which we have left unexplained. It cannot be undertaken here, but, briefly indicated, it involves a study of the Stoic attitude toward style from its original protest against any other conception of language than as a servant of thought, to its gradual recognition of the psychological justification of considerations of a sensuous and emotional character.

One other point should be noted. As I have suggested above that the figures of language and of thought were an important factor in giving theoretical definition to two types of *rhetorical* style, so it should be pointed out that the simple enunciative form of language ($λόγος\ ἀποφαντικός$, which is $ἀσχηματισμένος$) is looked upon as the normal type of the *plain* style. Indeed, the significance of the figures, and especially of the figures of thought,

---

[1] The Peripatetic Mean of Style, etc. A. J. P. XXV (1904) p. 140.

for ancient theories of style can scarcely be exaggerated. Some phases of the subject I shall revert to at another time.

The styles are not originally thought of as types of individualism (χαρακτῆρες), but rather as aspects of oratorical language as a whole, which in any ideal sense will combine with the language of emotion passages of exact reasoning and objective presentation. But as the one aspect would prevail over the other according to individual temperament and ability, so the elements of an abstract analysis of λόγος came to be looked upon as marks of individuality, that is, χαρακτῆρες, and thus passed into the service of literary classification or criticism. This development is, in fact, attested by our record, since, as we have seen, in the earliest example of the developed doctrine of the style (the Rhetorica ad Herennium) all three forms are thought of as an essential part of every stylistic product, and furthermore they are designated not as χαρακτῆρες but as σχήματα (figurae). A perfect synthesis of the two elements of logical exactness and emotional effect would not naturally often be found. But Dionysius believed that such an embodiment of the two main aspects of style was to be found in Demosthenes, and to the synthesis of them he gives the name of the middle style. The interpretation was inspired by a superficial conception of the Peripatetic idea of the μεσότης,[1] but it was misleading and has been the chief source of the mistaken conceptions of the matter which now prevail.

The whole subject may be summarized by saying (with the qualifications which I have indicated in the preceding study) that the grand style is rhetoric itself in the original conception of it as an instrument of emotional transport (ψυχαγωγία), the plain style is dialectic, the middle style a *tertium quid* intermediate between them. The history of rhetoric has many modifications of this simple underlying conception to record, but the only one which need be recalled here is the fact that the rhetorical style was further differentiated into two forms, the one of stylistic finish and elaboration (cultus), the other of vehemence and passion (vis). From the recognized pre-eminence of Demosthenes the latter type more and more usurped the designation of the grand style, while the former came to be known as the middle style.

G. L. HENDRICKSON.

[1] As I have explained before, A. J. P. XXV (1904) p. 145.

Sandys (John Edwin). Harvard Lectures on the Revival of Learning. Cambridge, *At the University Press*, 1905.

Schiche (Theodor). Zu Ciceros Briefen. Berlin, *Weidmannsche Buchhandlung*, 1905. 1 m.

Schlicher (John J.) The Moods of Indirect Quotation. Reprinted from American Journal of Philology, Vol. XXVI, No. 1. Baltimore, *The Friedenwald Co.*, 1905.

Schoenfeld (Hermann). Bismarck's Speeches and Letters. New York, *D. Appleton & Co.*, 1905.

Schultz (Wolfgang). Pythagoras u. Heraklit. (Studien zur antiken Kultur. Heft 1.) Leipzig u. Wien, *Akademischer Verlag*, 1905.

Shin Koron (The). Vol. XX, Nos. II, III. With a supplement by Kinza Hitai: A Vocabulary of the Japanese and Aryan Languages hypothetically compared. Tokyo, 1905.

Shorey (Paul). The Unity of Plato's Thought (The Decennial Publications of the University of Chicago). *University of Chicago Press*, 1903.

Tamil Language, A Handbook of the Ordinary Dialect of the. By G. U. Pope. Part III. A compendious Tamil-English Dictionary. Seventh Ed. Oxford, *At the Clarendon Press*, 1905. 5s. net.

Thiele (Richard). Schülerkommentar zur Auswahl aus Ciceros Rhetorischen Schriften. Leipzig, *G. Freytag*. Wien, *F. Tempsky*, 1905. geb. 1 m. 60 pf.

Thukydides. Erkl. v. J. Classen. XI. Band. 6. Buch. Mit 2 Karten v. H. Kiepert. 3. Aufl. Bearb. v. J. Steup. Berlin, *Weidmannsche Buchhandlung*, 1905.

Trendelenburg (Adolf). Erläuterungen zu Platos Merexenus. Berlin, *Weidmannsche Buchhandlung*, 1905. 1 m.

Vergils Aeneide. Textausgabe für den Schulgebr. Leipzig u. Berlin, *B. G. Teubner*, 1905. geb. 2 m.

Wenger (Karl). Historische Romane deutscher Romantiker. Bern, *A. Francke*, 1905. 3 fr. 50.

Wheeler (Benj. Ide). The Whence and Whither of the Modern Science of Language. University of California Publications. Classical Philology. Vol. 1, No. 3, pp. 95-109. Berkeley, *The University Press*, 1905. 25c.

Wilser (Ludwig). Die Herkunft der Baiern mit Anhang: Stammbaum der langobardischen Könige. Leipzig u. Wien, *Akademischer Verlag für Kunst u. Wissenschaft*, 1905.

Wisén (Magne). De Scholiis Rhetorices ad Herennium. Holmiae, MDCCCCV.

Wünsche (Aug.) Die Pflanzenfabel in der Weltlitteratur. Leipzig u. Wien, *Akademischer Verlag für Kunst u. Wissenschaft*, 1905.

CORRECTION.—Little did I think when I commented some years ago on the lapse of an eminent scholar, who confounded Strepsiades and Pheidippides (Curtius, Studien, I 2, 275), that one day some editorial Puck would get astride of my pen and make me write 'Acharnian' for 'Megarian', as happened in the last number of the Journal (p. 242, l. 5). In my handwriting, it is true, Acharnian and Megarian are not so far apart, but I will not saddle printer or proofreader with my inadvertencies. Nor will I say that to the Greek scholar the error corrects itself, as the dialect is Megarian. Else Professor HUMPHREYS would not have called my attention to the matter. μετὰ καὶ τόδε τοῖσι γενέσθω.

www.ingramcontent.com/pod-product-compliance
Lightning Source LLC
Chambersburg PA
CBHW070921180426
43192CB00038B/2152